WOMEN
beginning and building a growing
REACHING
women's enrichment ministry
WOMEN

Compiled by Chris Adams
Foreword by Anne Graham Lotz

LifeWay Press
Nashville, Tennessee

ISBN 0-7673-2593-1
Printed in the United States of America

Dewey Decimal Classification: 248.843
Subject Heading: CHURCH WORK WITH WOMEN \ WOMEN--RELIGIOUS LIFE
This book is the text for course LS-0034 in the Adult Leadership and Skill Development
diploma plan in the Christian Growth Study Plan.

Unless otherwise indicated, Scripture quotations are from the Holy Bible, *New International Version,* copyright ©1973, 1978, 1984 by International Bible Society.

Scripture quotations marked NASB are from the NEW AMERICAN STANDARD BIBLE.
© Copyright The Lockman Foundation, 1960, 1962, 1963, 1968, 1971, 1972,
1973, 1975, 1977, 1995. Used by permission.

Scripture quotations marked NKJV are from *The Experiencing God Bible* copyright © 1994 by
Broadman & Holman Publishers from the *New King James Version.* Copyright © 1979, 1980,
1982, Thomas Nelson, Inc., Publishers.

LifeWay Press
127 Ninth Avenue, North
Nashville, Tennessee 37234

Contents

Meet the Writers

Anne Graham Lotz
Anne, founder of AnGeL Ministries, travels across the world as a featured speaker at conferences, seminaries, churches, and universities. She also serves on the Board of Directors for the Billy Graham Evangelistic Association. She makes her home in Raleigh, North Carolina.

Chris Adams
Chris is the Women's Enrichment Ministry Specialist for the Discipleship and Family Division of the Baptist Sunday School Board, Nashville, Tennessee.

Susie Hawkins
Susie speaks frequently for women's conferences, retreats and Bible studies. She teaches a weekly businesswomen's Bible study called Focus and participates in various ministries at First Baptist Church, Dallas, Texas.

Esther Burroughs
Esther serves as Assistant Director, Field Staff, in the Church Growth and Associational Evangelism Department of the North American Mission Board, Alpharetta, Georgia.

Monte McMahan Clendining
Monte is currently serving with her husband Pat as an International Service Corp volunteer with the International Mission Board in Europe.

Valerie Howe
Valerie is a Family Ministry Special Worker for the Women's Ministry Division of the Missouri Baptist Convention. She resides in Lebanon, Missouri.

Rhonda H. Kelley
Rhonda is Associate Director, Innovative Evangelism; Adjunct Professor, New Orleans Baptist Theological Seminary; and Consultant, Ochsner Clinic and Alton Ochsner Medical Foundation Hospital, New Orleans, Louisiana.

Jaye Martin
Jaye is the Minister to Women at First Baptist Church, Houston, Texas.

Merci Dixon
Merci is Director of Women's Ministries at Moss Bluff First Baptist Church, Moss Bluff, Louisiana.

Gerry Sisk
Gerry is Women's Ministry Director/Women's Counselor at First Baptist Church, Snellville Georgia.

Foreword

Anne Graham Lotz

One of the most thrilling stories in all of Scripture is recorded in the book of Exodus when God saw the misery of His people enslaved in Egypt, heard their cries, and raised up Moses to liberate them from bondage and lead them to the promised land (see Ex. 1–14). God confirmed Moses as His liberator by demonstrating His power again and again through the plagues and the parting of the Red Sea. However, the apostle Paul tells us that two men, Jannes and Jambres, actually defied God by opposing Moses (see 2 Tim. 3:8). While we are not given the specifics, Jannes and Jambres must have opposed Moses by confronting the people with the choice of an alternative to God's prescribed way of liberation. And because God's way of liberation was the true way out of bondage, any alternative would lead not to liberation, but to destruction.

This is of special interest to those of us involved in ministering to women today, many of whom live in various types of bondage. God has seen the misery of their lives, He has heard their cries of emptiness,
of loneliness,
of meaninglessness,
of fearfulness,
of hopelessness.
And God has raised up His own Son, Jesus Christ, to liberate them from bondage, and lead them to an abundant life of satisfaction,
joy,
purpose,
fulfillment,
peace,
and hope.
But the apostle Paul indicates that in the last days there will be a unique attack on women similar to Jannes and Jambres (see 2 Tim. 3:6-9). The implication is that in the last days women will be attacked by being confronted with

an offer of liberation that opposes God's chosen Liberator, Jesus Christ (see John 14:6). Even though God has demonstrated His power again and again in the life of Christ, confirming once and for all through His death and resurrection that He is indeed God's prescribed way of liberation, women today are being deceived by alternatives. They are constantly being bombarded by voices that promise to lead them out of bondage and misery. But the promised liberator is not Jesus Christ, it is a professional career,

or an educational degree,

or financial prosperity,

or material accumulation,

or a marital relationship,

or maternal fulfillment,

or sexual pleasure,

or physical beauty,

or a famous reputation,

— the list of alternatives is almost endless.

While these choices confronting women today seem modern, the enemy behind them is ancient. He is trying to lure them away from God's Liberator with an offer of an alternative that will lead them to destruction. Tragically, the statistics on ...

abortion,

child abuse,

adultery,

abandonment,

alcoholism,

drug addiction,

depression,

and divorce

give silent witness to the effectiveness of the enemy's tactics.

My prayer is that God will use this book, and the women's ministries established, equipped, encouraged, and enabled by it, to help women resist the enemy's attack. I pray God will open the eyes of women everywhere to the Liberator Who has given His life to set them free from spiritual, emotional, social, and psychological bondage. And I pray women will then choose the only way to true liberation by placing their faith in Jesus Christ as their own personal Savior, surrendering to Him as Lord, and serving Him as King.

Introduction

What makes a swan beautiful? The color of its feathers, its beautiful long neck, and the graceful way it glides across the lake.

What makes a woman beautiful? Is it the color of her hair, the shape of her eyes, or the complexion of her skin? These things are only temporary. What truly makes a woman beautiful is who she is in Christ. As Christ enters a woman's life, something beautiful is created within that cannot be changed by earthly things. As a woman grows to become a disciple, there is an assurance, a hope, and a peace that only comes from the Lord.

Women Reaching Women was written in response to what is happening today across the country among women in churches. Perhaps you, too, have sensed that God is at work in a mighty way among women. Maybe that is why you are reading this book.

In *Experiencing God,* Henry Blackaby writes: "We tried to find out what God already was doing around us. We believed that He would show us where He was at work, and the revelation would be our invitation to join Him. We began praying and watching to see what God would do next in answer to our prayers."[1]

Women's leaders have prayed, watched, and seen God at work in hundreds of grass roots women's ministries across the United States. Over the last several years, scores of women have asked for help and resources. Their requests have all been the same: "We are hungry for information and direction." They have asked, "Can you help us?"

God has definitely been at work among women of all denominations during the past few years. This revelation became the invitation to join Him in the important work reflected in this book. Thus, Women's Enrichment Ministry was born.

Women's Enrichment Ministry has sought to help churches begin and build women's ministries by providing resources, training, enrichment events, consultation, and a supporting network. Responding not only to the needs of women but desiring also to utilize the spiritual gifts of Christian women, Women's Enrichment Ministry encourages women in spiritual growth, discipleship, enrichment, ministry, and evangelism. This ministry continues the historical involvement of women in the church, builds on the biblical principles of women as gifted for ministry, and expands the philosophical perspective of women ministering uniquely to women.

Women's leaders have prayed, watched, and seen God at work in hundreds of grass roots women's ministries across the United States.

Throughout history, women have played an important role in the work of the church. The Bible records Sarah's commitment to the Lord (Gen. 11:29–23:20). The distinguished judge, Deborah, exercised uncommon leadership over the people of Israel (Judg. 4:4–5:31). God provided the great king David through Ruth, a faithful Gentile woman who was devoted to her mother-in-law Naomi's God (Ruth 1–4). Hannah's faith in God gave her a much desired son, Samuel, whom she dedicated to the Lord's service (1 Sam. 1:8-28). Her godly life influenced Samuel as he grew to become a spiritual leader.

Scripture records that women were prominent in the New Testament as well, especially in the ministry of Jesus. In contrast to the society of His day, Jesus recognized the value of women and often chose to minister to them. For example, there was Peter's mother-in-law (Mark 1:30-31); the widow of Nain (Luke 7:11-15); and the crippled woman (Luke 13:10-17). Jesus included women in His miracles and often referred to them in His parables or teachings about spiritual truths (Matt. 25:1-13; Luke 18:1-8). Several women ministered to Jesus (the woman in Bethany, Matt. 26:6-13; Mary, Luke 10:38-42; Joanna and Susanna, Luke 8:1-3), while other women witnessed His resurrection (Matt. 28:1-8; Mark 16:1-8; Luke 24:1-12; John 20:1-9).

Women were also influential in the early church. First century women were active in public worship and in many aspects of church ministry. The apostle Paul ministered with Euodia and Syntyche (Phil. 4:2-3); Persis (Rom. 16:12); and Tryphena and Tryphosa (Rom. 16:12). In addition, women hosted church meetings (Lydia, Acts 16:14-15; Priscilla, Rom. 16:3-5), taught the faith (Lois and Eunice, 2 Tim. 1:5), provided support (Phoebe, Rom. 16:1-2), and colabored in ministry (Mary ministered with Paul, Rom. 16:6; also Junias, Rom. 16:7). The role of women in the local church has maintained its importance through the centuries. While society has changed its view of women over time, Christian women have always provided significant ministry in the body of Christ.

For many years, women have been involved in missions education. For example, the Woman's Missionary Union of the Southern Baptist Convention began in 1888 with a three-fold purpose: to learn about missions, to do missions, and to support missions. The original purpose of WMU was reaffirmed in recent years in a mission statement: "To provide missions-related programs, information, resources, and training to motivate and enable churches and believers to meet spiritual, physical, and social needs, locally and globally." Many churches include this missions organization in their total church program. In October 1995, WMU made significant changes in order to revitalize its missions program.

During the 20th century, women in many local churches recognized the need to branch out beyond missions and began to include other ministries. Several Protestant denominations, especially churches on the West Coast, began formal work with women. In the late 1970s and early 1980s, women's ministry groups emerged in churches because of the spiritual hunger of women for in-depth Bible study and personal prayer. This grass roots movement primarily focused on Bible study and special events. Presently many churches have organized women's ministry groups, developed budgets, planned programs, and hired staff. Women today are involved in all aspects of the church through staff positions, key leadership roles, and specific committees.

While society has changed its view of women over time, Christian women have always provided significant ministry in the body of Christ.

In the ministry of Jesus and the early church, Christian women performed vital ministry. In the contemporary congregations of today, women continue to perform vital ministry. Therefore, we must provide training and resources for women in today's local church if we want to join God in His movement among women. This handbook is one such resource: *Women Reaching Women* for Christ and discipling women in Christ. That is the basis upon which this book was compiled.

You obviously have a heart for ministry to and with women or you would not be interested in this book. Our hope is that through the contents of each chapter you will see God's hand at work in the women in your church. As you study, dream God's dream for your women. Let the Holy Spirit guide as you seek to follow where He leads.

---

[1]Henry Blackaby and Claude King, *Experiencing God: Knowing and Doing the Will of God* (Nashville: LifeWay Press, 1990), 66.

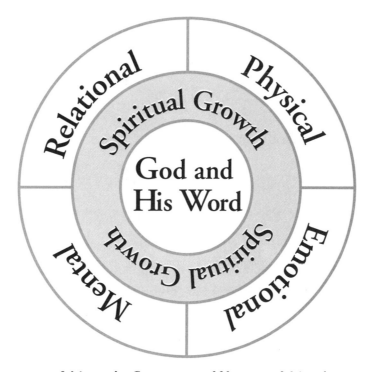

Women's Enrichment Ministry Wheel

All ministry must be centered on God's Word and our relationship to the God of the Word. Spiritual growth must be the ultimate goal of each of the spokes: relational (social, family, communication, witnessing, service, fellowship), physical (health, nutrition, addictions), emotional (self-esteem, depression, crises counseling), and mental (decision-making, time management, finances, leadership skills).

Why Have a Women's Enrichment Ministry?

Chris Adams

Several years ago God began stirring my heart in the area of reaching and discipling women. At the time, the only thing we had specifically for women in my church was a weekly Bible study and a missions group. While these effectively met the needs of the small numbers of women who attended, the majority of women were not involved. God increased the burden within me, "How can we reach all our women and encourage them to grow and follow Christ daily?" Three other women and I began praying, asking God what He would do to expand the ministry our church offered women.

Because there was not much available to help us develop a new and different ministry, much of what we did was trial and error and with continual prayer! We looked to see what other churches were doing to reach women. We visited and spent time with women's ministry leaders, picking their brains and learning from their experiences.

After many months and years of hard work, some mistakes, much prayer, and a willingness to "color outside the lines," we watched God develop a multifaceted women's enrichment ministry. We saw women who never thought of themselves as leaders begin to boldly take responsibilities and positions to serve the Lord. We also saw women come to know Christ, and others to base their entire lives on God's Word.

What a privilege to be a part of the Lord's work, to minister to and alongside women, to share what God has done in my life as He uses it to touch and change someone else. Women today need to know faith truly works, no matter what the world tells them. They need to know how to stay faithful in a world that has gone crazy and forsaken Christ.

For believers, ministry is not an option. Ministry is our responsibility. God calls each of us to serve Him. God empowers us and gifts us to accomplish what He calls us to do.

For believers, ministry is not an option.

Women Are Qualified to Minister

Women are qualified to minister to others for a variety of reasons. Both the Old and New Testaments provide examples of women who were a part of God's ministry. In the Old Testament Ruth chose to follow and minister to her distraught mother-in-law Naomi, as they grieved the loss of husband and son. In 2 Timothy we find Lois and Eunice, Timothy's mother and grandmother, passing along their heritage of faith. Dorcas (see Acts 9) was a woman who served both in her church and community, ministering to the less fortunate. The example of Jesus also qualifies women to minister. He spent His years teaching to meet spiritual needs and touching to meet emotional and physical needs. Jesus ministered to and with women throughout His earthly ministry.

Redemption and giftedness are additional qualifications that inspire women to be busy about the Lord's work. Because of our salvation, we have the gift of life to share with the world. Because of our personal giftedness (see 1 Pet. 4:10), we are equipped to serve Christ each day as He leads. It is both a privilege and responsibility to use the gifts God has given us. Since Jesus has commanded that we "go and make disciples," (Matt. 28:19) how can women NOT minister? The only prerequisite is that they have experienced life—the joys, trials, victories, and sorrows—and that they are willing to share transparently what God has done through each experience.

Leadership skills develop as women boldly step out in faith to attempt the great tasks God assigns to them.

Leadership skills develop as women boldly step out in faith to attempt the great tasks God assigns to them. For example, a woman I know had never felt qualified to accept a position of leadership in her church. After attending a women's Bible study, she realized God had given her gifts to use for Him. She had never seen herself as talented and felt as if she had little to give back to Christ. When a leader invited her to take part in planning a women's retreat, she accepted, even though she felt inadequate. She learned from the others on the retreat committee as they spent time in prayer and preparation. She learned the importance of serving and giving others the opportunity to serve. Eventually this woman became a ministry leader in her church. When God moved her family to a new city, she was prepared to share her gifts and experiences to help develop a women's enrichment ministry at her new church.

Reasons for Having a Women's Enrichment Ministry

Do you have a vision for reaching women and discipling them for life change? Is God stirring the hearts of the women in your church, creating within them a hunger for serving Christ? Are they seeking to know Christ more intimately, to serve Him more faithfully, to share their faith with those who need a Savior? Are you prepared to lead them as they seek to grow spiritually?

An exciting thing is happening in many of our churches. I continually receive calls from pastors and women's ministry leaders who say, "There seems to be a movement of God among our women. God is at work in their lives, and we want to be ready to respond."

Women desire to reach out to hurting women as well as disciple them. Women have a deep spiritual hunger to know Christ and experience Him personally. They want to know how to survive in a world that has gone crazy. They want to know how to balance responsibilities and live a full and meaningful life.

Many church leaders have attempted to develop women's enrichment ministries. They ask, "What can we do to help? How can we reach women whose needs are not already being met by other ministries in our church? How can we minister to these women and disciple them so that they become all God desires them to be — serving Him faithfully in their families, professions, churches, and communities?" These leaders seek to reach women for Christ, disciple them, and equip them to reach others. Women's ministry was born on the grass-roots level to meet these needs.

Men cannot meet all the needs of a woman; women need relationships with other women. They need godly role models; wiser, more spiritually mature women after whom to pattern their lives. The Bible says in Titus 2:3-5, "Likewise, teach the older women to be reverent in the way they live, not to be slanderers or addicted to much wine, but to teach what is good. Then they can train the younger women to love their husbands and children, to be self-controlled and pure, to be busy at home, to be kind, and to be subject to their husbands, so that no one will malign the word of God."

Women's enrichment ministry is not a stand-alone program but a piece of the puzzle that makes up the body of believers.

Because they no longer live close to their families, many younger women need mentors who will encourage and teach them. They need someone who has been there to say "I understand, and I'll pray with you through this," or "Here is how God spoke to me as I was experiencing the same thing." Brenda Hunter quotes her friend Ree, "A mentor comes alongside, puts her arm around you, and says, 'You can do it.' "[1] A mentor does what Paul asked Timothy to do, "And the things you have heard me say ... entrust to reliable men (and women) who will also be qualified to teach others" (2 Tim. 2:2).

An effective women's enrichment ministry is not a stand-alone program in the local church, but actually a piece of the puzzle that makes up a body of believers. In carrying out their purpose, women support the purpose of the entire church. A women's enrichment ministry can create synergy that comes from the unique ministry to and with women as it addresses their unique needs. Because of the diversity of women, a ministry to women must be diverse in content, options of activities offered, time of day conducted, and day of week held. The individual needs of both professional women and full-time homemakers must be addressed. We must consider the unique needs of empty nesters, singles, senior adults, and single mothers. As we do, we can develop ministry to help each woman accept and love who God created her to be and provide encouragement for her to grow in her relationship to Christ, fellow believers, and a lost world.

As we began to develop our women's ministry, we looked at the women, their lifestyles and life phases, their needs, and their gifts and talents. We offered large-group Bible study and worship one morning a week to draw all kinds of women together for fellowship and discipleship. There was also an evening Bible study geared to women employed outside the home. Elective courses were part of each semester's studies including discipleship studies such as *Experiencing God, The Mind of Christ, First Place, WiseCounsel*; marriage, homemaking, and parenting studies; crafts and aerobics classes; community ministries such as a soup kitchen and clothes closet; mission studies and participation; and prayer groups. Special events were planned each quarter and monthly noon luncheons were offered for all women. This diversity enabled us to reach a larger number of women.

Today's woman lives in a world that tells her she can have it all, do it all, and be "super woman" through it all. Many women feel guilty because they cannot accomplish this in their personal, professional, and spiritual lives.

If today's woman reads secular publications and watches television, she is bombarded by humanistic answers to her needs. When that does not work, where will she turn? Will this woman, who is desperate for relationships and attention, find a support group of like women to help her walk with Christ daily? Will she be challenged in her spiritual life to spend time with God in prayer and to dig deep into His Word to find answers? What a challenge for us as women's ministry leaders! What a responsibility! What an opportunity!

Why have a women's enrichment ministry? For the same reasons we have single adult, senior adult, children's, youth, or men's ministry. First, to meet the unique needs of the target audience. In this case, the target audience is women of all ages and all walks of life. And second, to encourage ministry as a way of life. All believers are called to minister and serve. In *Experiencing God: Knowing and Doing the Will of God,* Henry Blackaby says you cannot be in relationship with Christ and not be on mission. Ministry emerges from our relationship with Christ.

Ministry emerges from our relationship with Christ.

Concerns About Women's Enrichment Ministry

Some people have the idea that women's enrichment ministry is only concerned with personal growth; learning but not applying that learning. This is not the case if the ministry is conducted appropriately. Effective ministries will lead women to seek God's Word, apply it, and share it throughout their daily living; to become "sold out" to Christ in every area of life; and to serve God with their whole heart. As that happens, they are unable to contain their joy in the Lord, and it spills over to all with whom they come in contact. Sharing their faith verbally as well as by lifestyle becomes a way of life.

A second common concern about women's enrichment ministry is that women participating in it will become a detached group, functioning on their own without the knowledge or support of the church staff. As leaders are trained to effectively relate to staff (see "Building Your Leadership Team," page 60), they share their burden and vision for reaching women and seek the staff's support and direction. They support the purpose of the church as a whole, not just women's enrichment ministry.

Benefits of a Women's Enrichment Ministry

There are a number of benefits that result from providing and supporting a women's enrichment ministry in the church.

1. Women grow in their relationship with the Lord.

It was through a young women's Bible study that I was first challenged to get up in the morning before my children woke to spend time in prayer and Scripture reading. It was truly a challenge. Not only was I tired most of the time, I don't even like to get up early when I am rested! But what a difference it made in my attitude and focus for the day as I reflected on the constant presence of the Lord in my life.

Women grow in their relationship with the Lord as they participate in study, prayer, and ministry to others. As women grow spiritually and learn how to minister, their families, church, and communities benefit.

2. The church grows numerically.

The church grows as participants in women's enrichment ministries seek out and meet the needs of women in their community with the message of Christ.

Janet would only live in our city for a few months while her husband was on a job site. She would then relocate to another location for a few months. She joined our church because our women's enrichment ministry offered her a place to study God's Word during the week and make friends quickly during the fellowship time before and after our study.

As women invite neighbors and coworkers to participate in women's studies and activities, prospects are discovered and encouraged to become a part of the church. I have seen members bring lost friends to one of our women's enrichment ministry activities, and they find Christ. In this way women encourage the body of Christ to grow.

3. New women find their niche.

A women's enrichment ministry draws in women who have recently joined the church to help them become familiar with and find their "niche" (area of ministry). In the church where I served, we began a New Shepherding Ministry that reached out to each woman who joined the church. Leaders of this ministry committed to having at least five "touches" with each woman to make sure she didn't slip through the cracks or leave through the back door of the church because she did not find her area of service or the place where her needs could be met. The "touches" included a visit to share information about the church, including ministry opportunities for women; an invitation to the next women's event (with a free ticket provided); a follow-up phone call to see if she had any questions regarding the church; or an invitation for coffee or lunch. We also made sure she knew where to find Sunday School classes for herself and her family members.

4. Meaningful relationships form.

A women's enrichment ministry opens the door for relationships between women from different backgrounds, ages, and life stages. Fellowship is one activity that seems to take place spontaneously when women get together. As the women's enrichment ministry of your church offers activities for all types of women, fellowship takes place automatically. As ladies study, pray, and worship together, lasting and meaningful relationships develop.

One of my closest friends was Delight Clark, a precious lady who shared my vision and burden for reaching and discipling women in our church. We spent much time praying, studying, and serving together. We grew in our love for each other. God planned for our relationship to be deeper than just planning a ministry at our church.

5. Women are encouraged to discover, develop, and use their spiritual gifts.

We are told, "As each one has received a gift, minister it to one another, as good stewards of the manifold grace of God" (1 Pet. 4:10, NKJV). Although each woman is gifted, she may not realize it, or may not know what her gifts are. Others know their gifts but do not understand how to use them to serve God.

For years after I became a Christian, I didn't realize God had gifted me to serve Him. I thought God skipped me when He handed the gifts out. As I began to study about how each believer is gifted (1 Pet. 4:10), I realized that included me. Organization has always been fairly easy for me. I thought everyone had a calendar, marked important items on it, and looked at it periodically so nothing would be missed. I discovered that is not necessarily true. Maybe the gift of administration was the gift I was to use in ministry. As I began to let God develop that strength in me, He opened doors and called me to serve. As I looked at the women in our church, I realized I was not the only one who did not understand what God's Word says about spiritual gifts. Through women's enrichment ministry, women can discern their gifts and find opportunities to use those gifts in service for the Lord.

6. Today's woman is ministered to.

Women today have almost no spare time and will only spend what little time they have on things worth the sacrifice they must make to be involved. The busy woman of today must feel the activity is something she needs to make a difference in her own life or in someone else's. We must offer study and ministry opportunities at various times throughout the week to accommodate women with different schedules, lifestyles, and family responsibilities. If we only offer a Tuesday morning discipleship study, what does that say to the woman who works Monday through Friday from 8:00 to 5:00? She may feel as though she is not important to you and your women's ministry. Where will she find a group of women with whom she can share, pray, and study? By providing a diverse schedule and diverse options for study, we let each woman know she is important to us and to God.

Busy women today will give of their time and energy if the activity makes a difference in their lives.

7. Coordination and organization are provided for inreach and outreach to women.

Often in churches there are various studies and activities but no central source of information. A structure of organization will provide a network of information so each woman knows what is available—studies that will help her grow in her relationship with Christ, ministries to meet her needs, service opportunities in the church, and outreach ministries to women in the community.

When we began to organize our women's enrichment ministry, there were several groups already established, but no one person really knew the details of each. There were many ministries (both within the church and in the community) where a woman could serve, but no place to find out all that was available. As we set up our structure, we listed all the opportunities a woman had for study and service, even if these were not just for women. We wanted to serve as a central source of information so each woman could discover ways she could participate throughout the church. This was especially helpful to new church members who were inquiring about opportunities for women.

8. Women receive woman-to-woman understanding and lay counseling.

This aspect of women's enrichment ministry will lighten the staff ministers' load at times when a woman really only needs someone to listen and share with, rather than a professional counselor. Women need women who can share emotions and experiences and help round out life's experiences. In her newsletter, *Just Between Us,* Jill Briscoe writes, "After all, who but a mother can fully empathize with a young woman who has suffered a miscarriage or struggled with being shut up with small children all day long? Who but a woman can sympathize with mercurial monthly emotions or PMS or the changes that come unbidden when we hit 50! What a wide open door our very sex affords us. We can walk right into the hearts and lives of half the human race and present Christ, all because we are female."[2]

I have a dear friend and mentor who shared her walk with the Lord with me in a way that greatly influenced my life. I had seen her struggle with a difficult family issue. She continually exhibited peace, joy, and incredible faith. Little did I know one day my family would experience the same type of struggle. What I had seen in her life, in her walk with the Lord, encouraged me to trust God. Often I would call her just to say, "Tell me again how you made it." What a comfort when she and other Christian friends called to say, "Our family has experienced what you are going through, and we are praying for you." Only someone who has been there can truly say "I understand." A woman dealing with crisis needs to know she is not the only woman to go through the same type of situation.

After praying and waiting for God's timing, our church established a lay counseling ministry for women. Counselors first trained by studying *Wise-Counsel: Skills for Lay Counseling* (see "Tapping Resources for Women's Enrichment Ministry," page 124). This study prepares women to listen, ask appropriate questions, and know when to refer for professional counseling. The name chosen for this ministry was "Heartstrings: Confidential Conversation for Women." Women who experienced difficult life situations and with the Lord's help "made it" were willing to listen and encourage women who are dealing with similar issues. There was a list of women who were "on call" if someone needed to talk to a woman who had been through what she was now experiencing. Names used for this ministry in other churches are "Care and Share," "Encouragement Network," "Called to Encourage," and "YokeFellow Ministry." The participation is temporary, not long-term, and each one ministered to is encouraged to use her experience to minister to another woman.

9. Older women mentor younger women.

Throughout a woman's life, she should continually look for someone to mentor—someone younger with whom she can share insights the Lord has given her. At the same time, each woman should be looking for someone to mentor her—a woman from whom she can learn about life and relationships. No matter where we are in age or spiritual walk, mentoring and being mentored should be a pattern we follow throughout life.

I have already told about some friends in my life who have mentored me spiritually. Another friend that God sent my way early in my marriage was Anne.

Women need women who can share emotions and experiences and help round out life's experiences.

She was an older lady who was a widow and had no children. She "adopted" my husband and me when we moved to her neighborhood in East Texas. My mother lived several hours away, and I could not pick up the phone and call her every time I had a domestic crisis in my kitchen. Anne filled the gap. She was the one I called almost daily with questions about homemaking. She taught me much about managing a home, loving my husband, and the importance of joining a local church. Anne knew it would impact our marriage, our children, and our lives. She is with the Lord now, but I still thank God for her friendship and her love for Him and for us.

10. Entire families are affected as women are drawn closer to the Lord.
When a woman is reached through women's enrichment ministry, her family is also touched. I have seen ladies whose marriages were transformed when they began to put Christ first in their lives. I have seen mothers become more at peace with themselves and their children as they discovered they were not alone in dealing with the daily work of preschool children or the difficulties of teenage years. I have also seen single women begin to trust God with their "singleness" as they learned from other singles that they are essential to the effective functioning of the body. When you influence a woman's life for Christ, you touch all those in her sphere of influence as she lives out her Christianity.

11. Women get help to fight spiritual battles.
All of us face spiritual warfare. It goes against the grain to walk a life of faith in Christ in this secular world. It would be all too easy to "shoot our wounded," but as women of God we must reach out and help restore lives. More than likely, each of us will need a hand at some point in our journey. We need to be willing to give and accept help to face the enemy whose goal is to destroy our Christian witness to the world.

Women need to stand alongside one another as they daily walk in a world that is in bondage to sin. When one woman is weak, she needs others to stand with her, encouraging her to be strong and pointing her to God and His Word.

The Tasks of Women's Enrichment Ministry

What should be the tasks of every women's enrichment ministry? Women's enrichment ministry exists to:
• *equip* local church women to enrich the lives of other women through Christ;
• *help* women discover their God-given gifts for ministry, determine needs in their communities, and match those needs with their gifts of service; and
• *lead* women to accept Christ as Lord, become women of deep prayer, and become women who study the Bible and base their lives on the Word of God.
The remainder of this book is devoted to achieving the tasks of women's enrichment ministry.

---

[1]Brenda Hunter, Ph.D., *In the Company of Women* (Sisters, Ore.: Multnomah Books, 1994), 182.
[2]Jill Briscoe, "A Letter from Jill," *Just Between Us: Jill Briscoe's Newsletter for Ministry Wives* (Jacksonville, FL.: Preaching Resources, 1990), n pag. (This resource is now a magazine published by Telling the Truth Media, Brookfield, WI, 1-800-260-3342).

Three Generations in the Here and Now

Susie Hawkins

Stephanie is a 23-year-old woman living in Dallas. She holds undergraduate and master's degrees and is employed as a financial consultant. When Stephanie was 12, her parents divorced, and she experienced some turbulent teenage years. Although she is skeptical about religion in general, she is involved in her community and attends church occasionally. In her free time, Stephanie enjoys entertainment, movies, sports, and is quite adept at surfing the Internet.

Stephanie's mother, Linda, is 48 and works as a successful real estate agent. She is remarried and is the stepmother of two teenage boys. In addition to these demands, Linda is responsible for the well-being of her widowed mother. She is interested in church activities as long as they don't require too much of her time or energy.

Marie is Linda's 74-year-old mother. She suffers from minor health problems and occasional bouts of depression. Marie is on a fixed income and often struggles to make ends meet. She is committed to her church and is faithful in her attendance and support at Sunday School, worship, and other activities.

These three women are bound together as a family, yet pulled apart by their own generational needs. How can a women's enrichment ministry in a local church effectively reach Stephanie, Linda, and Marie? Understanding the generational differences that pull these women apart is a key to reaching women in the 21st century.

Our Emerging World

As we seek to develop women's enrichment ministries that are effective, we must understand the times in which we live. A host of recent books describe life in the United States and the Western world at the turn of the millennium. They refer to this as a transition period from the modern worldview to the postmodern worldview.

Gary McIntosh, in his book *Three Generations: Riding the Wave of Change*, says that our "failure to understand and respond to the changing generational influences in the United States may have negative impact on our churches and ministry."[1] McIntosh suggests five potential results:

1. A slow decline for many local churches and related denominations.
2. Fewer recruits for missions with a resulting loss of influence on unreached peoples.
3. Less money with which to finance missions or other local church ministries.
4. A continual trend toward the liberal agenda in the United States.
5. An inability to fulfill our God-given purpose to "make disciples of all nations" (Matt. 28:19).[2]

McIntosh identifies three broad generations of people in the United States today. He refers to the Builder Generation, people born before 1946, the Boomer Generation, people born between 1946-1964, and the Buster Generation, people born between 1965-1983.[3] Other researchers identify additional segments, but we will use these to help us understand and respond to the world in which we live.

The Builder Generation

Like Marie in our opening example, anyone born before 1946 is included in the Builder Generation, although this is a much broader period than the 20 to 25 years usually associated with a generation. Using the middle range of U.S. Census Bureau population projections as of July 1, 1996, there were 69,152,000 Builder Generation people residing in the United States.[4] The Builder Generation may be subdivided into the G.I. Generation (pre-1925), the Silent Generation (1926-1939) and the War Babies (1940-1945).[5]

The Builder Generation went through turbulent periods in American history—World War I (1914-18) the Roaring '20s, the Great Depression (1929-39), World War II (1939-45), and the Korean War (1950-53)—that threatened it from within and from without. In the United States, this generation moved from a rural lifestyle in an isolationist society to the leading urban-oriented, military, industrial, economic, and cultural influence in the world during the period from the 1920s to the 1950s. Builders experienced deprivation and rationing during the Great Depression and World War II, and developed an early love affair with the automobile that gave them a sense of independence and power.

Three institutions formed the center of life for Builders: family, school, and church. "The process of becoming an adult was carefully supervised by these three institutions. Social activities revolved around church and school activities. Family, school, and church most often worked together to build a fairly stable life, which helped people face difficult times and created a sense of unity. Couples rarely divorced. Fewer diversions meant that husbands and wives had more time for each other. Few women worked outside the home, so divorce, even in an unhappy marriage, was usually not an option for women. Traditional values permeated the home, community, and nation."[6]

The Builder Generation includes anyone born prior to 1946.

Today, Builders generally believe in the worth of the "traditional" family. George Barna defines the traditional family as "people who are related to each other by marriage, birth, or adoption. The married couple without children, the married couple with children, parents and their adopted or natural children, and extended families (grandparents, parents, children, aunts, uncles, nephews, cousins) could all fit into such a category."[7]

They are a Make-do Generation that has found through their churches faith, encouragement, and support during difficult times. Builders grew up and received training in Sunday School and church. Sunday School and church attendance continue to permeate their lives. Even if their motive may not be spiritual, they attend because of social commitment. McIntosh says, "Builders … have a strong sense of obligation to serve the church. They are often at the heart of their churches, in part due to their dedication and willingness to serve. They are the most church-going generation, and they give graciously to charities — especially religious organizations."[8]

In churches, Builders were trained to answer ministry needs with structured programs overseen by committees and boards following denominational models. This generation has a tremendous sense of denominational loyalty and commitment. For them, Sunday School, corporate worship, and missions programs came to be modeled after denominational patterns. "For Builders, corporate worship is a time of quietness and contemplation of God. A worship service that requires minimal audience participation and that includes hymns, expository or content-oriented sermons, a pastoral prayer, recognition of guests, and organ/piano music is preferred."[9]

The Boomer Generation

The Boomer Generation includes anyone born between 1946 and 1965.

Babies born between 1946 and 1965, like Linda, comprise the Boomer Generation. Using the middle range of U.S. Census Bureau population projections as of July 1, 1996, there were 83,101,000 Boomers residing in the United States.[10] "The Boomer Generation can be divided into two primary groups: the Leading Edge—those born between 1946 and 1954—and the Trailing Edge—those born between 1954 and 1964. … There are roughly 34 million people who are Leading-edge Boomers (LEBs). … The second half of the Boomer Generation, born between 1955 and 1964, is called the Trailing Edge. There are about 42 million in this group." This period witnessed the first time over 50 percent of American households had television sets (1954) and saw the introduction of the polio vaccine (1955).[11]

Boomers were deeply influenced by the events of the Cold War and the launching of the first man-made space satellites—Sputnik I and II—launched by Russia before the first American satellite—Explorer I—was launched on January 31, 1958. In addition to various crises of the Cold War, Boomers were heavily influenced by television in the 1950s. Programs like "Leave It to Beaver," "Father Knows Best," "Make Room for Daddy," and "Ozzie and Harriet" were popular programs for Leading-edge Boomers. Trailing-edge Boomers were influenced even more by television and such programs as, "Happy Days," "One Day at a Time," and "The Brady Bunch." Television brought common interests to Boomers regardless of their economic or social lines.[12]

The economic boom following World War II set off unprecedented economic expansion in the United States. Median family income rose from $5,000 during the 1950s to over $6,000 during the 1960s. This increase in median family income was directly linked to the double-income family, where both husband and wife worked outside the home. This redefinition of marriage and family stands as the most significant difference between the lifestyle of the Builders and the Boomers.[13]

Twenty-five years of results from an increased median income, two-parents working, soaring divorce rates, etc., have caused Americans to redefine the meaning of "family." Today they often identify the family as "nouveau" (nü-vō′) instead of traditional. According to Barna, "the nouveau family can be defined as two or more people who care about each other. The individuals need not be related by marriage or other legal bonds, nor even be living together. What must be true of them, instead, is that they demonstrate, either tangibly or intangibly, a significant degree of mutual care or concern."[14]

Accompanying the economic impact on the family was the Sexual Revolution that liberated the American woman both publicly and privately. "Beginning in the 1960s, traditional sexual and cultural attitudes in America came under fire. Birth control, child care, sexual equality, working women, 'no-fault' divorce, legalized abortion, interracial marriages, and unwed mothers" helped make alternative families (the nouveau family) respectable in the eyes of many.[15] Barna observes,

> The breakdown in sexual morality that occurred in the 1960s was the consequence of a more serious breakdown in thinking about the truth. … The biblical view of truth posits that the ultimate authority in all matters of life, including family, is a matter of absolutes, not a matter of choices. Truth is not one of several alternatives one might or might not embrace according to one's personal preference. For many years this thinking about truth was reflected in the moral standards considered generally acceptable throughout the country and in legislation proposed and enacted. But over time, a pluralistic view took over. It posited that the ultimate authority was self, mediated by society and its laws. Whereas religious beliefs may inform some of the family-based decisions people make, neither the Bible nor any other religious-based teaching is considered inerrant.[16]

The Boomer Generation has largely ignored the church, except for baby dedications, weddings, counseling, and funeral services. They are less involved with the institutional church than Builders, and moving about every third year they usually change religious affiliation at least once. This has been a factor in the decline of mainline denominations. Boomers exercise their newly obtained sense of liberation by controlling and directing their lifestyle agendas. Linda, in our example, and other Boomers invest their money in highly-relational causes they can observe firsthand rather than traditional church programs they cannot evaluate personally. They expect tangible results for their investments, and they tend to support projects and people who are close to home. Boomers view themselves as problem solvers and usually respond to their own interests rather than to a sense of responsibility that interferes with their individual lifestyles.[17]

The Boomer Generation generally spent much of their time experimenting—with drugs, causes, communes, music, religion, Eastern and New Age practices, and self-help philosophies. They tend to see things in shades of gray rather than black and white. They have greater tolerance for different viewpoints, lifestyles, ideals, and even contradictions.[18] Many adults who rejected essential religious beliefs are making their way back through non-Christian religions. "In place of the traditional Sunday morning routine, many opt for personalized exercises in spiritual exploration and development. Sunday School, midweek services, and evangelistic crusades are being replaced by more intimate gatherings, such as small groups that meet for discussion, Bible study, and prayer; house churches; and worship festivals."[19] Churches expecting the same programs and styles of instruction they had been using for years and years to satisfy the spiritual needs of young adults have learned their methods are unsuccessful. "After a five-year period of experimentation, Boomers have been departing from churches in record numbers, starting in the early nineties. When churches offered only pat answers to increasingly complex issues, Boomers took their quest for spiritual enlightenment elsewhere."[20]

Because of social, economic, cultural, and family pressures, Boomers are pulled in directions unlike any faced by the Builder Generation. This often leads to a breakdown of communication between the two generations. Builders, for example, find it difficult to understand how Boomer priorities and schedules cause them to seek a more convenient form for expressing their corporate worship, study, and ministry experiences.

The Buster Generation

Stephanie and other babies born between 1965 and 1985 comprise the Buster Generation. Using the middle range of U.S. Census Bureau population projections as of July 1, 1996, there were 74,041,000 Busters residing in the United States.[21] Among the many names used to identify the Buster Generation, one of the most common is Generation X, from Douglas Coupeland's 1991 novel. George Barna labels the teenage half of this generation as Generation Next.[22] One feature about the Buster Generation is that there are more males than females in each of the five-year age groups for the first time in this century.

Influences on Busters include the Roe -vs- Wade decision by the U.S. Supreme Court in 1973. The growth in technology has been another major influence. "Between 1946 and 1960 the number of computers grew from 1 to 10,000. From 1960 to 1980 to 10 million. By the year 2000 there will be over 80 million computers in the United States alone."[23] Video games, television, videotapes, mobile telephones, and other high tech innovations have helped change the face of world culture. The flood of information predicted by Alvin Toffler in *Future Shock* in 1970 has arrived like a gigantic tidal wave.

On January 28, 1986, the space shuttle *Challenger* exploded moments after lifting off. In 1989 the Berlin Wall was torn down and Communist regimes were dramatically dismantled. Operation Desert Storm (1991), lasting less than 100 hours, brought Star Wars technology to new levels of awareness. AIDS (Acquired Immune Deficiency Syndrome), first diagnosed in 1981, quickly rose to pandemic proportions around the world. Drugs, crime, violence, and even

The Buster Generation includes anyone born between 1965 and 1985.

suicide spread across American culture. Many Busters responded by rejecting the promiscuity practiced by Boomers and expected to be a part of their culture. For Busters the "quality of life" is serious business.[24]

Busters argue "about the ethics of information privacy on the Internet (the telecommunications network that connects all on-line computer users, a veritable Infobahn ['Information Superhighway'] of the age). They're engaging in verbal warfare about human dignity, personal responsibility, and the lifestyle implications of globalism. They converse about quality of life as a matter of course. They know more about family structures and influence than we ever dared to contemplate. They may not be as well-schooled or even as articulate as our [Boomer] generation was, but today's youth are not idiots. They are more experienced, more thoughtful, and less driven to conquer the world than we were at their age. That in itself speaks volumes about their intelligence and maturity."[25] They are characterized by six S's: they are serious about life, stressed out, self-reliant, skeptical, highly spiritual, and survivors.[26] The following list indicates life conditions Busters consider desirable.[27]

Having good physical health 90%
Having close personal friendships...84%
Having a comfortable lifestyle 82%
Having one marriage partner for life 80%
Having a clear purpose for living 79%
Having a spouse and children..69%
Living with a high degree of integrity 61%
Having a high-paying job...60%
Having a close relationship with God 58%
Having a satisfying sex life with a marriage partner 57%
Influencing other people's lives...53%
Making a difference in the world 53%
Living close to family and relatives...44%
Owning a large home..37%
Being personally active in a local church 37%
Achieving fame or recognition 21%

Stephanie, in our example, and other Busters view the world through post-modern eyes. They don't readily accept a belief in the infinite-personal creator God of the Bible. For them, knowledge and reason are uncertain. They are more subjective than they would like to admit, and their religious commitment has been privatized to the extreme. To them, truth is relative and not absolute, since it is governed by people who are social beings in various social settings that influence the meaning of words used to communicate ideas.

Unlike Boomers, Busters haven't ignored the church nor its programs. They have, however, a sharply modified view of what is important. Like the Builders, Busters recognize the value and importance of formal gatherings of the church. However, the components of public worship, education, and fellowship are different. Busters prefer that their worship and training leaders come down to their level rather than appear as authoritative resource persons. They opt for an informal, even casual, setting. Regardless of the setting, Busters strive for relationships. They nurture one another and seek to walk together in their spiritual commitment. These radically different styles often leave Builders in disarray.

Before we consider a ministry to the generations of Marie, Linda, and Stephanie, let's summarize in chart-form Builders, Boomers, and Busters.

Getting It Together[28]

General Traits

	Builder	Boomer	Buster
Aliases	Strivers Survivors Suppies (senior, urban professionals) Opals (older people with active lifestyles) Rappies (retired, affluent professionals) War Babies (born 1940-1945) G. I. Generation Silent Generation Seniors	Yuppies (young, urban professionals) Oinks (one income, no kids) Dinks (double income, no kids) New Collars (information workers) Gold Collars (highly paid information workers) Postwar Babies Postwar Generation Vietnam Generation Sixties Generation Thirtysomethings and Fortysomethings Challengers Me Generation	Yiffies (young, individualistic, freedom-minded, and few) 13ers (13th generation from the founding fathers) Twentysomethings Tweens (young Busters on the verge of being teenagers) Posties (Post-Boomer generation) Generation X Echo Boom Baby Boomlet The Reagan Generation
Formative Years	1920s, 1930s, 1940s	1950s, 1960s, 1970s	1980s, 1990s, 2000s
Formative Experiences	World War I Roaring Twenties Great Depression Rural lifestyle Automobile Radio The New Deal Big bands Pearl Harbor and World War II Rationing Korean War Family, school, church	Cold War Television Economic affluence Education and technology Rock and Roll Civil Rights movement The new frontier Space race Assassinations Vietnam War and Kent State Energy crisis Watergate and Nixon resignation	*Roe -vs- Wade* High technology Video games and television The *Challenger* disaster Berlin Wall dismantled Peer groups and work Music, music, music Variable economy Persian Gulf War AIDS Clinton administration
Characteristics and Concerns	Hard workers Savers Frugal Patriotic Loyal Private Cautious Respectful Dependable Stable Intolerant	Educated Media-oriented Independent Cause-oriented Fitness conscious Enjoy rock music Action-oriented Desire quality Question authority	Freedom Sixties nostalgia Community causes Feel neglected and lonely Willing to work Reject Boomer values Want practical education Postpone marriage

Religious Traits

	Builder	Boomer	Buster
Religious Characteristics/ Involvement	Committed to church Support foreign missions Enjoy Bible study Loyal to denominations Minister out of duty Worship in reverence	Committed to relationships Want to belong Supportive of people Want to live their faith Want experiences with faith Tolerant of differences	Committed to family Local causes Shorter attention span Want up-to-date options Want faith that meets needs Want less structure Need to relieve stress

Ministry	Provide group activities	Highlight purpose and vision	Define vision
	Sunday school	Use celebrative worship	Update worship service
	Mission projects	Stress quality	Focus on local issues
	In-depth Bible study	Streamline structure	Short-term service
	Focus on marriage and grandparenting	Offer multiple options	Use small groups
		Use small groups	Answer questions
	Encourage contact with other generations	Restructure existing services	Develop need-based ministries
		Communicate visually	
	Offer pastoral care	Expand roles of women	
	Challenge them to pass on leadership	Focus on local ministry	
		Offer short-term missions involvement	

Common Areas of Concern	Finances	Spiritual search	Sports and fitness
	Affordable housing	Desire to return to traditional values	Friends and family
	Personal safety		Entertainment and music
	Continued health	Slower lifestyle	Improving the environment
	Adequate transportation	Second career development	Search for serenity
	Preparation for death	Finances	
	Spiritual needs	Reevaluating goals	
	Retirement options	Midlife transitions	
	Substance abuse education	Preparing for retirement	
	Elder abuse education	Death of the American Dream	

Reaching the Unchurched	Set up hotlines	Emphasize family	Become Buster-friendly
	Provide support groups	Develop bridge ministries	Value Busters
	Schedule traditional activities	Offer a seeker service	Start a seeker service
		Stress lifestyle evangelism	Preach "how to" messages
	Help with Social Security and income taxes	Provide quality child care	Establish new ministries
		Give opportunities for service	Provide parafamily structures
	Sponsor trips	Welcome guests appropriately	
	Offer classes	Create opportunities for belonging	Teach life skills
	Offer counseling		Be involved in the community
	Train for grandparenting	Minister to singles	Host large group activities
	Be clearinghouse for Builder needs	Get involved in the community	Schedule retreats
		Plant a daughter church	Stress marriage and family
	Offer respite care		Communicate your vision
			Offer time and space

Ministering in a Meaningful Way

Scripture tells us to "walk circumspectly, not as fools but as wise, redeeming the time, because the days are evil" (Eph. 5:15-16, NKJV). Our "time" is one of those momentous periods of transition in human history. We are experiencing a "paradigm" (active example, pattern) shift involving the First Wave (agrarian), Second Wave (industrial) and Third Wave (technological). The paradigm shift also involves tensions between modern and postmodern worldviews.

In the midst of this paradigm shift, there is a common thread that binds together Builders (grandmothers), Boomers (mothers) and Busters (daughters) regardless of their ethnic or economic circumstances. This element provides the incentive for reaching women for Jesus Christ.

The common thread that will help us reach out to Marie, Linda, and Stephanie is their basic personal spiritual need. Our Lord has charged us with the commission to "go and make disciples of all nations" (Matt. 28:19-20). When we help women come to a personal relationship with Jesus Christ, this basic spiritual need will be met — initially. From that point on we have the opportunity to draw them into an awareness of their place in God's family.

For women, the most effective way to meet their spiritual needs with God's solutions is by establishing meaningful relationships within the Body of Christ. This principle is drawn from Scripture. The apostle Paul wrote of the common

The common thread that will help us reach Builders, Boomers, and Busters is their basic spiritual need.

faith for all generations when he said of Timothy, "I thank God, whom I serve, as my forefathers did, with a clear conscience, as night and day I constantly remember you in my prayers. Recalling your tears, I long to see you, so that I may be filled with joy. I have been reminded of your sincere faith, which first lived in your grandmother Lois and in your mother Eunice and, I am persuaded, now lives in you also" (2 Tim. 1:3-5).

How this is accomplished is bidirectional. From Stephanie's and Linda's perspectives we learn to "Give proper recognition to those widows who are really in need. But if a widow has children or grandchildren, these should learn first of all to put their religion into practice by caring for their own family and so repaying their parents and grandparents, for this is pleasing to God" (1 Tim. 5:3-4). From Marie's and Linda's perspectives we are told to "speak the things which are proper for sound doctrine … the older women likewise, that they be reverent in behavior, not slanderers, not given to much wine, teachers of good things — that they admonish the young women to love their husbands, to love their children, to be discreet, chaste, homemakers, good, obedient to their own husbands, that the word of God may not be blasphemed" (Titus 2:1-5). Taking Marie, Linda, and Stephanie by the hand we, as Christian leaders, must draw them into maturity through our relationship with them and with our Lord. By precept and example, we can teach them the importance of Christian fellowship both personally and corporately.

Stay in Touch

Women today differ from their mothers and grandmothers in lifestyles, activities, and nonchurch backgrounds. How can we reach them for Jesus Christ? How can we train and develop them as Christians to walk with the Lord, with their families, and in their communities? To achieve this we need to discover who women are and what they expect as we enter the 21st century. We must also consider some demographic data related to income level, occupations, families, divorce, remarriage, age ranges, health issues, and survival rates of women entering the new millennium. Let me give two examples of helpful sources.

We need to discover who women are and what they expect as we enter the 21st century.

- *American Demographics: Consumer Trends for Business Leaders* publishes articles in market research designed to help this Dow Jones Company plan for its business activities in the United States. Periodically it releases interim reports of official U.S. Bureau of Census information on population to provide important portraits relevant to American life and society at this junction of two millennia. Check your library to access this information.

- *The Internet* provides a multitude of sites where information and studies about women may be found. Surfing the Internet reveals widespread issues confronting women at the turn of the millennium. Professor Cindy Suerkeck of Vanderbilt University in Nashville, Tennessee, listed 24 major categories (with numerous subcategories) of women's issues resources in May 1996. At that time she requested input on how to link to even wider areas that cover the broadest possible spectrum of interests. In June 1996, one of the top five sites on the Internet was "Women's Wire" guide to sites.

Christian leaders need to become aware of these and other tools and use them to help reach and disciple women to come to Jesus Christ and His church. There is no shortage of information available. Resources abound on every hand! As a women's enrichment leader, search for the latest information and utilize it in planning for and ministering to women in the 21st century.

[1]Gary L. McIntosh, *Three Generations: Riding the Waves of Change in Your Church* (Grand Rapids: Fleming H. Revell, 1995), 19-21.

[2]Ibid.

[3]Ibid., 26,75,130.

[4]U.S. Bureau of Census, Current Population Reports, Series P25-1130, "Population Projections of the United States by Age, Sex, Race, and Hispanic Origin: 1995 to 2050."

[5]McIntosh, 26-27.

[6]Ibid., 36.

[7]George Barna, *The Future of the American Family* (Chicago: Moody Press, 1993), 26.

[8]McIntosh, 45.

[9]Ibid., 48.

[10]U.S. Bureau of Census.

[11]McIntosh, 76-77.

[12]Ibid., 78-80.

[13]Ibid.

[14]Barna, *The Future of the American Family*, 26.

[15]Ibid., 33.

[16]Ibid., 33-34.

[17]Adapted from McIntosh, 95-99.

[18]Ibid.

[19]Barna, *The Future of the American Family*, 188.

[20]Ibid.,189.

[21]U.S. Bureau of Census.

[22]George Barna, *Generation Next: What You Need to Know About Today's Youth* (Ventura, CA: Regal Books, 1995), n. pag.

[23]McIntosh, 133.

[24]Ibid., 133-143.

[25]Barna, *Generation Next*, 17.

[26]Ibid., 19-21.

[27]Ibid., 28.

[28]The substance of these tables is drawn from McIntosh, 69-70,124-126,165-167.

Women Using Their Gifts ... to Share The Gift

Esther Burroughs

Growing up with five brothers and sisters, my home was certainly a place where lessons were taught and learned. My mother once gave my older sister a small handful of candies, telling her to divide them with her brothers and sisters. My sister carefully counted them out. The numbers did not come out evenly. My mother watched as my sister pondered a minute. She saw a look come over my sister's face as she thought of the solution. She promptly ate enough candy to make the number come out evenly—and then she shared with us what was left! That was not exactly fair, and certainly not the way our Heavenly Father gives gifts to His children.

Another childhood memory is the time I stayed with my maternal grandmother as we waited for her son, my uncle, to come home from the Navy. I swung on the fence gate, waiting each day, hoping he would come. When the day finally came, he picked me up and carried me down the cinder sidewalk to my grandmother's house. He had a gift for me. He put his hands behind his back and asked me to choose. No matter which hand I chose, he would give me the gift anyway. Perhaps this looks more like God's gift giving; the gift is always there because God does not trick us. James 1:17 says, "Every good and perfect gift is from above, coming down from the Father of the heavenly lights, who does not change like shifting shadows." Just imagine, being given a gift by the One who never changes! This is great news in our changing times. No matter how we respond, the Giver of the gift never changes.

Kingdom citizens live with this radical truth! God's gift of salvation and subsequent spiritual gifts are not based on our acceptance or rejection, our worthiness or unworthiness, our temperament, or our personality type—all of which the culture deems important. God's gifts are based solely on His unchanging, gift-giving love. Our culture bases much of its behavioral values upon the gifts they receive and the gifts they are able to give. We, as the body of Christ, have the gift our culture needs, and it is our challenge to accept, develop, and share Christ through our spiritual gifts, showing the culture the way. We must do that as leaders and challenge the women we lead to do the same.

God Is Creator

We must first embrace the truth that we are made in the image of God and created with a purpose. Paul's words in Ephesians 1 tell us how blessed we are. We have our inheritance in Christ Jesus. We are chosen, holy, blameless, adopted, redeemed, and forgiven, according to the riches of His grace. We are blessed with every spiritual blessing in Christ Jesus. What is His is mine, because I am His. God's words to us are like the Father's words to the elder brother, "My son, you are always with me, and everything I have is yours" (Luke 15:31).

Women of our generation can help women of the next generation realize that acceptance depends not upon the world's standard, but on Christ's. "God created man in His own image, in the image of God he created him; male and female he created them" (Gen. 1:27). Verse 31 says, "God saw all that he had made, and it was very good." We are "very good" in the estimation of God.

Jesus claimed His birthright and His position as the Son of God. Jesus' mission was to die on the cross, taking our place, exchanging love, and giving us new birth. Jesus came to show us what God, His Father, looked like. Jesus asks us to claim our birthright in Him and live in such a way that others know we are His.

Jesus said to His *parents*, "I must be about My Father's business" (Luke 2:49, NKJV).

Jesus said to *His disciples,* "Don't you believe that I am in the Father, and that the Father is in me? The words I say to you are not just my own. Rather, it is the Father, living in me, who is doing his work" (John 14:10).

Jesus says to *us,* "[You] will do even greater things than these" (John 14:12).

During Jesus' earthly ministry, He showed the world what God is like in human flesh. Several years ago, singer/songwriter Amy Grant sang a song titled, "My Father's Eyes." The words challenged the listener: "as the world looks at me, let them see My Father's eyes." Just as Jesus did His Father's work and modeled for the disciples what that looked like, He calls us today, created in His image, to imitate God the Father. We can do that by keeping our eyes on Jesus.

At family reunions you will hear remarks like, "She has her mother's eyes" or, "He is just like his grandfather."

While visiting my oldest granddaughter, she said, "Nana, just look! My mother's hands are just like yours." Then she looked at her own hands and said, "And my hands look just like my mother's. WOW, Nana!" She was correct. My daughter has my hands and eyes. Her three daughters have her hands and eyes. One of the miracles and joys of grandparenting is seeing the grandchildren and recognizing the family likeness. That is both frightening and exciting!

We are children of the Heavenly Father—with His family resemblances. Does our Heavenly Father delight in our looking like Him? To be made in His image is an awesome privilege and responsibility. Perhaps heaven will be like a family

We must first embrace the truth that we are made in the image of God.

reunion where everyone notices how much each of us resembles our Heavenly Father. I believe we image our Father when we accept our position in Christ, claiming our kinship, and remembering Whose we are. Give thanks to your Creator Father, and ask Him to help you grow to look more like Him. In Ephesians 5:1 Paul says, "Be imitators of God, therefore, as dearly loved children."

God Is Gift Giver

Psalm 139 identifies our uniqueness. God is omnipresent and omniscient.

Oh Lord, Thou hast searched me and known me.
Thou dost know when I sit down and when I rise up ...
Even before there is a word on my tongue,
Behold, O Lord, Thou dost know it all.
Thou hast enclosed me beyond and before,
And laid Thy hand upon me.
Such knowledge is too wonderful for me (Ps. 139:1-2,4-6, NASB).

Romans 11:33 tells us what Paul believes about this creator God.

Oh, the depth of the riches of the wisdom and knowledge of God!
How unsearchable his judgments,
and his paths are beyond tracing out!

Even in our computer world, and even with word search, nothing can compare to the unsearchable ways of God.

The Psalmist also says there is no place we can go to escape God. I love the line, "Darkness is as light to you [God]" (Ps. 139:12). When women go through dark times or situations in their lives, they can cling to the fact that nothing has changed with God. He is light and in Him is no darkness. The Psalmist continues,

I praise you because I am fearfully and wonderfully made;
your works are wonderful,
I know that full well (Ps. 139:14).

With the Psalmist we must declare, "How precious to me are your thoughts, O God! How vast is the sum of them!" (Ps. 139:17). Imagine a God whose thoughts about us outnumber the very sand of the sea. That is a thought worthy of our praise and adoration.

We accept that the God of creation is our Creator, and He intimately knows us and calls us into a personal relationship with Himself. From that intimacy, we share the gifts He has given us with the body of Christ, which will impact our world and the kingdom of God.

God's Spirit Empowers the Gift

In his book *Mirror, Mirror on the Wall*, Ken Hemphill says, "Spiritual gifts are individualized endowments of grace from the Father, equipping you to play a vital role in His plan for the redemption of the world."[1] Consider characteristics of gifts that need to be shared with your women.

The Holy Spirit Reveals the Gifts

At the very moment you accept Jesus Christ as your personal Savior, the Holy Spirit enters your life, giving you gifts. That is referred to as the baptism of the Holy Spirit. The baptism of the Holy Spirit is a one-time experience. But the filling and empowering of the Holy Spirit is a continual process. Without this continual filling, our gifts would be powerless. The Holy Spirit gives specific gifts to every believer (see Eph. 4:1-16). No one is left out.

Prayer Is the Key in Discovering Gifts

Ask God to reveal your special area of giftedness. Ask other persons in the body of Christ to pray with you to help you discern your personal gifts. As you pray, don't be afraid to try different things in the body of Christ which will help you discover your gifts. Teach preschoolers, work with teenagers, or share in a Meals-on-Wheels program. Through prayer and the use of your talents, the Holy Spirit not only helps you recognize your gifts, but also helps you develop these gifts.

The Body of Christ Grows Stronger as Gifts Are Used

We are to exercise our gifts in the body of Christ—for the body of Christ. As you share your gifts with others, ask yourself: *Am I making myself look better, or the body of Christ look better?* The gift is not regarded as a spiritual award, but it is God's means for service and ministry. We must give the gift back through the body of Christ.

In 1 Corinthians 12, Paul paints an amusingly profound word picture of the body of Christ. He says the body has many members. Every member has a function and is a vital part. He reminds us that no part is better than any other part. No part is greater than any other part. All parts of the body are needed for the body to be complete, to properly function, and to fulfill its purpose in the kingdom of God. The reason for your spiritual gifts is the building of the body of Christ through the ministry of your gifts, which brings glory to the Father in His plan of redemption.

Too many Christians today are doing jobs in the body of Christ without exercising their gifts. The body of Christ will look healthy when each part is fulfilling its purpose, exercising individual gifts, and not just filling positions. There is nothing more exciting than watching a Christian use his or her gift in the body of Christ, and watching how that enhances and impacts the whole body, and ultimately the kingdom. Your spiritual gifts energize you and others in the body of Christ. When I am the recipient of another's gift, I am drawn to Christ and encouraged in my faith. When I share my gift in the body, I sense the Spirit and the power of God working through me, and find it humbling beyond explanation. It is in no way prideful or an attempt to draw attention to myself. Rather, I feel utter dependence upon the Gift Giver, and know that without His touch, I have nothing to share. It is God's gift; it is His kingdom. Don't waste a moment desiring another's gift. Work hard to develop the gifts God has given you for the purpose of making the body stronger.

"You are exactly who God designed you to be. Your function is vital to the body because God made you just as He desired."[2]

Work hard to develop the gifts God has given you.

Gifts Are Given Out of God's Grace.

Paul points to the work of the Spirit by repeating phrases such as "same Spirit," and "one Spirit" (see 1 Cor. 12: 4,9). In verse 4 Paul uses the word that comes from the Greek root word for *grace,* and can be translated *manifestation of grace.* Paul would have us understand that our gifts were given because of God's grace, not for our boasting. When I think of the manifold grace of God, I think of a pleated skirt. There is pleat after pleat after pleat, as if there were no beginning or end. God's grace is like that; many-folded, unending grace.

The Scripture theme for Women's Enrichment Ministry is taken from the New King James translation of 1 Peter 4:10, "As each one has received a gift, minister it to one another, as good stewards of the manifold grace of God." The Father would have us accept our gifts from Him, always aware that He is the Giver, we are the receivers, and in obedience, we share the gifts with the body of Christ to bring glory to God through the body of Christ, His church.

Affirm and Celebrate Each Other's Gifts.

Recently, I was preparing to speak to a very diverse group of women. I was given careful instructions on theme. In my preparation, I looked at 1 Corinthians 12. I had read it many times, but on this day the Holy Spirit highlighted it for me. "There are different kinds of gifts, but the same Spirit. There are different kinds of service, but the same Lord. There are different kinds of working, but the same God works all of them in all men" (1 Cor. 12:4-6). *WOW!* How can I question or critique another's gift when the same Spirit gave gifts to all? How dare we not affirm and celebrate each other's part in the body!

Learn to Accept Each Other's Gifts.

We cannot exist alone, for we are dependent on each other. Women need to learn to accept each other's gifts, knowing each gift is placed in the body for the purpose of ministry. We will look more like Christ as we celebrate these gifts and our places in God's family, desiring the family portrait to look more like Christ. No matter how significant you might think your gift is, its only significance is found as a part of the whole body of Christ.

We cannot exist alone, for we are dependent on each other.

When we understand that different gifts in the body are given by the same Spirit—all for the purpose of God's love redeeming the world—we take the focus off ourselves and our gifts and place it properly at the feet of Christ. We are stewards of the gifts, not owners. You are Christ's body—that's who you are! Never forget this. Only as you accept your gift-part of that body does your gift-part have meaning. If today's church is to make any difference in the world in which we live, the whole body of Christ must put aside labels, idioms, and programs, join hands, and imitate Christ to our culture—for the purpose of redemption of the world.

Women are caregivers by nature, but we can go a step further. We can affirm, encourage, and help develop the spiritual gifts in others, empowering them to exercise their God-gift in and through God's family, the church.

Take time to read 1 Corinthians 12. It is so enlightening. Read just a bit more and see chapter 13 through the eyes of chapter 12. You will have a better understanding of how God calls His body to live.

- We *never* look more like Him–than when we use the gifts He has given us.
- We *never* look more like Him–than when the gifts of the body bring glory to Christ.
- We *never* look more like Him–than when the body, the church, reaches out to become Christ in everyday living because we are *Kingdom Citizens*.

Our goal in any kind of women's ministry should simply be: *Women gifted by the Holy Spirit … empowered by the Holy Spirit … ministering to one another … as good stewards of the manifold grace of God.*

God Compels Us to Use Our Gifts

Our spiritual gifts are to be used to minister to others in the name of Christ to touch our world. The amazing thing about giving away your gift is that the giver and the receiver are both blessed. The old saying *what goes around comes around* is true. Let me share some true-life stories that may trigger an idea or two for your women's ministry.

In giving away your gift, you and the receiver are both blessed.

The Gift of Hospitality

A church in the western part of the United States designed a dinner event through the membership of the church to intentionally reach the unchurched in their community. Two or three couples would plan to get together for dinner. Each couple shared in the preparation—from cleaning the house to preparing and serving the food. This way the work of hospitality was shared.

Hospitality is difficult today with the schedules we have to keep. What a great idea! It is always more fun to plan an event with others. Each couple invited unchurched friends from the neighborhood or workplace to the special dinner. With two or three couples, the conversation flowed easily.

Later in the year, the dinner event was planned again. This time, the couples exchanged responsibilities and again invited their unchurched friends. By now, they knew each other's interests, and it became easier to share about their relationships to Christ.

Later in the year the church hosted a banquet, featuring good entertainment and a special guest speaker. Once again, the unreached friends were invited as special guests. At the end of the message, an appeal was given to anyone who might be interested in finding out more about a relationship to Christ. In the first year of this event, 80 people came to know Christ. That, my friends, is kingdom living—sharing the gift of hospitality to share *The Gift*.

The Gift of Listening with the Heart

I heard of a pastor's wife who makes her way to meet the neighbors each time her family moves into a new community. After introducing herself, she offers a Saturday morning play time for their children to join her children in their home. She tells her neighbors she will tell the children Bible stories, help them do crafts, and play games with them.

What mother would not allow her children to have two hours of entertainment like this on a Saturday morning? This pastor's wife shared her gift of love for children to impact God's kingdom. When I heard this, I was stunned. My children are grown, but when they were little I invited their friends over to play often. But, to be honest, I never thought of it as a time to share Bible stories!

Think of the impact this kind of event could make in today's world with so many mothers working outside the home. Think of single mothers and single fathers who need this gift. Before you say you don't have time for this, think about it. By exercising your gift with children and practicing this gift on a regular basis, you might develop a neighborhood ministry. Remember: gifts are not for you, they are for God. How wonderful for the children of single moms or dads who don't have time for such wonderful Saturday morning or after-school activities where they can experience God's love through a neighbor. It seems to me this kind of caring, nurturing gift would make the kingdom of God look different in that community and more inviting to the neighbors.

I am convinced that if we would refine our gift of listening—listening with the heart—we would have opportunity to share Christ more often. Look at the people in today's world. All around you see tired faces, stooped shoulders, tears, anger, and loneliness. Is your spiritual gift listening? You could change the kingdom of God with a listening heart.

If we would refine our gift of listening with the heart, we would have opportunity to share Christ more often.

The Gift of Being Yourself

I was headed for a weekend speaking engagement for high school girls. We experienced airplane trouble, and received the famous line: *We're sorry for any inconvenience we've caused you.* When we finally boarded the plane, I knew I would not make it in time to speak. God's provision is always ample; the missionary on the program could take my place. We were 45 minutes into the flight when the pilot said, "Ladies and gentlemen, we have an indication that there is a problem with the left engine, so to make sure everything is alright, we are heading back to Atlanta. *We're sorry for any inconvenience we've caused you.*"

As the passengers left the plane, many began attacking the ticket agent. A women standing by me began literally eating cigarettes, not smoking them! She would put one in her mouth, bite it, and throw it down. Somewhat out of control, she began to rant and rave about not getting back on the plane. She grabbed me by the arm, asking me how to get to a bus station. I was dressed in red and black that day, so I guess she thought I worked for the airline! I looked up the phone number and gave it to her.

I sat down by her and began trying to calm her down. As we quietly talked, she said, "Well, what's wrong with you anyway?"

"Nothing," I responded.

"That's what I mean," she said. "Why are you so calm?"

I explained that I was on my way to speak to a group of teenage girls about the most important relationship in my life. I'm not sure if she was interested in what I was saying or if what I was saying took her mind off that plane! I continued to share with her my relationship to Jesus Christ and how that made a difference in my life. About that time, a man whom I had never seen before tapped me on the shoulder, saying we could get rebooked through Charlotte and I could go with him to the ticket counter. I do not usually go with strange men, but I told him I would go. As I closed my conversation with the woman, she had calmed down. I wished her well.

As I walked away, I stopped to compliment the ticket agent on the way she had handled the crowd. I asked for her name and badge number so I could write the airline about her good work. She was stunned by my remark, and said, "You just made my day! Thank you!"

You see, being gifted in the body of Christ simply means using our spiritual gifts in the most natural way. Being courteous, listening, looking up phone numbers, being calm in the chaos of life, giving the world a glimpse of part of the body of Christ—impacting the kingdom of God with the secret weapon of spiritual giftedness! Oh, by the way, the man I mentioned earlier said to me as we walked away, "I'm a deacon at a church here in this city. I prayed for you as I heard you share Christ with that woman." Yes!

The Gift of Grace

A CEO of a successful company recently found herself in the employee workroom. She discovered a huge mistake had been made by her employees which would cost the company an enormous amount of money. The CEO raised her voice, jumping all over the supervisor and the other people at fault. Leaving them, she walked back into her office and slammed the door, rattling the windows and pictures, and feeling a bit justified in her actions. She later told me, "After settling in my office and reflecting on what had happened, I remembered that God was my CEO, and He would not have been pleased with my actions."

She went back to the workroom and apologized to the supervisor for her remarks and apologized to the others. Back in her office once again, her office door opened; the supervisor peeked inside and said, "I guess this Christian thing does work after all." Once more, the kingdom looked more like Christ because of the obedience of one part of His body that displayed the spiritual gift of grace.

Oh, women, this giftedness in Christ is so much bigger than our individual gifts, though the spiritual body is not complete without our gifts. We are part of something much bigger than ourselves. It takes every gift and every part being everything we can to make the body look more like Christ. When one part (like that CEO) makes a difference, the whole body looks good. When one part fails to use his or her gift, the whole body fails. What an awesome thought. You don't live unto yourself, for you are part of something much bigger. My prayer is that you will take seriously the issue of your gift-part of the body of Christ and challenge the women in your women's ministry to do the same. Waste no time or concern about another person's gifts, except, of course, to encourage them. Consider instead the heavy realization that without every part being its best, the whole cannot be complete. It will not bear the family resemblance of Christ as it should. We are kin by the blood of Christ, and a family must act like a family, knowing what it cost God to make us His family.

The Gift of Bible Teaching

I was lying on the table having a sonogram. I glanced at the calendar and said to the nurse, "That's the wrong date on your calendar. I only know because today is my 35th wedding anniversary."

"Wow," she replied. "How have you stayed married that long?"

Being gifted in the body of Christ means using our spiritual gifts in the most natural way.

I replied with a grin, "I'm sure it's because we have worked hard at it and had lots of help from Christian friends, family, and the church."

The nurse shared that she was a new Christian. Being a woman, I wanted the details. Being a woman, she gave them! Because of the recent events in the Middle East, many people on the hospital staff were asking, "Who are the Jewish people?" As a result, a doctor offered his gift of Bible teaching at noon on Thursdays to anyone on the staff who wanted to attend. This nurse asked Christ into her heart because of that Bible study. She went on to tell me that before the Bible study was over, 19 people in that hospital had accepted Christ. One doctor shared his gift of teaching, and the kingdom of Christ looked different—because one part of the body exercised its spiritual gift.

When we use our spiritual gifts, we show a life invested in kingdom authority.

The Gift of Witnessing

I have a dear friend who has a talent for quilting. She is quite remarkable. Her home is like a museum; her quilts enhance the warmth of her home. She also has the gift of evangelism. While living in Utah, she invited her Christian friends for coffee one day. She showed them the quilts she had designed based on hymns that told the story of her spiritual journey with Christ. Prior to her friends leaving, she told them, "I want you to pray for me next Friday because I am inviting my Mormon neighbors to my house, and I'm going to share my testimony with them. I was just practicing on you." See what happens when we use our gifts to share the Gift? We show a life invested in kingdom authority.

The Gift of Sharing a Talent

I know of a woman who was a career model, before she married and had a family. As her daughter entered the teen years, she and her daughter planned a sleep over. The daughter baked the refreshments and prepared for guests. Invitations were sent to school and church friends. The mother gathered the makeup, mirrors, and accessories. It was a wonderful evening of fun, learning how to present oneself in the best possible way. What encouragement to those young ladies whose mothers perhaps did not have that gift. What a gift from mother to daughter, taking the time and love to show how important it is to take care of one's body. It was natural for the mother in conversation through the evening to share about inner beauty and God's desire for our hearts to belong to Him. Another part of the body, through family, giving a gift, touching His kingdom.

The Gift of Being Part of the Family of God

I got on the motorized cart in the Dallas/Fort Worth Airport to go from Gate 3 to Gate 33. A priest got on at the next stop. Looking at me, he asked, "Is Dallas your home?" "No," I responded, thinking I would tell him where I lived. Before I could complete my sentence, he said, "It's not mine, either. Mine is Cloud 22." I then replied, "If yours is 22, then mine is 23." He reached out giving me a high five and said, "Then praise God! You must know Jesus." There we were, total strangers until that exchange of information, now celebrating the gift of the family of God while tooling through the Dallas airport in a motorized cart, high-fiving about Jesus! Everyone on the cart heard our testimony. We were kingdom living.

The Result of "Gift Giving"

I often say in my seminar, "We can live in the expectancy of what the Holy Spirit will do through gifts and obedience as we share Christ in the everydayness of living."

Several years ago, I came to know that my mother's brother, the one who gave me gifts as a little girl, did not know Christ and was deathly ill. I was so saddened. Mother told me that my father had shared Christ with my uncle many times, but he always responded that he was just not ready.

I promised my mother I would join her and my aunt in praying for Uncle Peter to know Christ. I learned from Oscar Thompson's book *Concentric Circles of Concern* to pray, " 'Lord, engineer circumstances in [Uncle Peter's] life to draw him to you.' "[3] As I began to pray, "God, manage the circumstance in Uncle Peter's life to bring him to yourself," I was led to write my uncle a personal letter, the first one in many years. I had just read a book about expressing yourself in word pictures to conjure up emotions and help the receiver accept the message. I did just that. I wrote all about being at my grandmother's home as a little girl. I reminded him of the old outhouse, complete with the Sears catalog; the crunching sound of the cinder sidewalk under our feet as we walked around; the gate upon which we used to swing and get in trouble; and the softness of my grandmother's comforting arms. I reminded Uncle Peter about the times he brought me small and simple gifts and how they were so appreciated. I then wrote, "Please forgive me that I have never shared with you the most important gift in all my life." I wrote out the Roman Road plan of salvation and the prayer to pray to receive Christ. I continued, "This is God's gift to you, Uncle Peter, and I will be praying that you will receive this gift." I never received a response, but I kept praying.

Sometime later, my aunt went to visit him one last time to share the gift of Christ. The nurse let her in. She told Uncle Peter why she'd come. He whispered, with a slight smile, "That's all settled. I got a letter from Esther." You see how God took different gifts in the body to bring a child to Himself? God used my father's consistent testimony. He used prayers, concern, letters, and caring relationships with my mother, her mother, Uncle Peter's sister, and his niece to love Uncle Peter into the kingdom. What a reunion we will have in heaven!

Let's go back to my precious granddaughter's realization that her hands looked like her mother's and her mother's hands looked like mine. Rightly so. That's family genetics. When people see you, do they see your Heavenly Father's eyes, hands, heart, and likeness? What imitation of our Heavenly Father are you currently living? Are you challenging the women in your women's enrichment ministry to do the same?

Gifted woman of God, with love and abandon, give the gift Christ has endowed to you to bring Him glory and to impact eternity.

Spiritual gifts are about kingdom living, family reunions, and celebration as the family of Christ.

What imitation of our Heavenly Father are you currently living?

---

[1] Ken Hemphill, *Mirror, Mirror on the Wall* (Nashville: Broadman Press, 1992), 13.
[2] Ibid., 62.
[3] Oscar Thompson, *Concentric Circles of Concern* (Nashville: Broadman Press, 1981), 77.

Beginning a Women's Enrichment Ministry

Chris Adams

In *Experiencing God: Knowing and Doing the Will of God,* Henry Blackaby says that we cannot stay where we are and go with God. That means we must be constantly changing, growing, and moving forward. In women's enrichment ministry it means we must be willing to obey God's calling to develop opportunities for service and growth, even if "we have never done it that way before."

With that attitude, how do we begin a women's enrichment ministry? Let me suggest a process.

Pray

The first thing you must do is pray. Your vision for women in your church and community must be God's vision or it will be on a shaky foundation. Through prayer you allow the freedom for God's Holy Spirit to guide all you do. Pray with a group of interested women to see where God is at work and how He wants you to join Him to develop ministry to and with your women. These women should be visionary (seeing with Christ's eyes) and have a ministry mindset (more concerned about people than programs). The focus is changing lives rather than creating programs. Some items to include in your prayer could be leadership, program options, moving the ministry from entertainment to discipleship, purpose, organizational structure, reaching more women for Christ through this ministry, and the staff person you will relate to. This could take a matter of weeks, months, or even as long as a year before you proceed to the next step. Then prayer must continue to be a thread woven into every area of this ministry to stay in tune with God's leadership.

Share Your Vision with the Church Staff

Share with your pastor or staff liaison your vision. Several pointers may help as you take this step.

1. Be specific, possibly presenting a one-page proposal listing goals and objectives for consideration.

2. Remember that it is your responsibility to contribute a female point of view to what may be an all-male staff.

3. Let the staff know that women's enrichment ministry is available to assist and help in all programs of the church.

4. Know and obey church policies concerning securing facilities, childcare, and publicity.

5. Listen to the staff. Ask their perspectives and expectations of women's ministry. Take interest in their areas of ministry. Learn from them.

Beth Smith, Women's Ministry Director at First Baptist Church, Orlando, Florida, asked her education ministers what their idea of women's ministry was. She asked their advice as she began planning. She also asked, "What can I do to undergird your area of ministry?"

6. If you attend a staff meeting, understand the rules. Ask questions ahead of time to understand what is expected during these meetings.

7. Choose the right time to address the pastor or staff. Ask for an appointment and let him know how much time you will need. Try giving back the last five minutes of that time. Your staff will appreciate that unexpected gift! You might even send a written list of questions ahead of time for his consideration.

8. Be specific and take a short list of issues to discuss. Remember to get to the bottom line quickly. Gary Chapman, associate pastor of Calvary Baptist Church in Winston-Salem, North Carolina, shared this statement in a women's conference: "Men speak in sentences and women speak in paragraphs." A church staff's plate is full already. Try not to add more than is absolutely necessary by giving details they do not need.

9. Turn in calendars early so the women's activities will not conflict with other church functions.

10. Ask the pastor's wife and/or other staff wife to serve as an advisor on your committee. She can contribute a staff wife's perspective on various issues, but do not expect her to attend or be involved in everything your women's enrichment ministry is planning.

11. If whatever you are desiring to do will hinder the church in any way—don't!

Network

Look beyond the borders of your church to see what others are doing to reach and disciple women. Begin to network with others who are involved in women's enrichment ministry in your community and state, both within and outside your denomination (see information on groups you can network with on page 125). Find out what is being done, what is working, and problems to watch for. Look for churches that have a well-developed ministry with women, and spend the day with the leaders. Call, write, and get together with those in the network you develop. Ask how they got started. What works in one church will not necessarily work in another, but giving and receiving ideas, resources, and information are great ways to stimulate thinking and guide prayer. Look together with other women's enrichment leaders for answers to common questions regarding women's ministry.

Networking with others will strengthen your ministry with women.

Assess Needs

With staff approval, the next step is to gather a group of women from all areas of your church, various ages and life phases, to comprise a "survey study team." These women should believe that God desires for women to know Christ personally and mature as believers. The purpose of this group is to decide on the type of survey (see Sample Questionnaire, page 46) to present to your women to identify their needs, availability, time preference for studies and ministry activities, child care needs, and other important information. No matter how meaningful the activities, if it is not what women want or need, they will not participate. Women today want choices, and they want to be asked, not told, what they need.

You must have a clear understanding of your church as well as your women and their needs to begin developing an effective women's ministry. Check to see what ministries are available through your church. Do not duplicate what is being offered. Instead, encourage women to participate in those ministries.

Develop a Purpose Statement

As you pray, meet together, and develop a survey, you should also be forming your purpose statement. This could be one sentence or a short paragraph that can be shared whenever you are asked what your women's enrichment ministry is all about. Your purpose statement should support the purpose statement of your church and should have a scriptural reference. All activities and plans should reflect this statement. If any plan does not support your purpose, you should question whether it is valid. You may choose to use in your statement words such as evangelize, encourage, fellowship, inform, teach, pray, worship, learn, glorify God, serve, minister, and involve in missions. The following are examples of purpose statements to help you get started:

• The vision of women's enrichment ministry is to seek to fulfill Christ's mission by encouraging women with a sense of belonging to God and each other, enabling women in becoming all they are to be in Christ, and equipping women for blessing others with the love, grace, and truth of Jesus Christ (Eph. 4:11-12).

• Women's Ministries Goals: Sharing Christ with those who do not know Him, strengthening Christians who do, and fervently praying for each ministry opportunity (Matt. 28:19-20).

• We purpose to keep balance between being ministered to and ministering to others, to confront women with the love of Jesus through outreach, to minister to the needs of our women, to help women develop their God-given potential as persons of value in their homes, church, and community, and to involve women in creative service under the leadership of the Holy Spirit (1 Cor. 14:26).

• The Women's Ministry is designed to meet the complex needs of today's woman. Women especially need one another's encouragement, prayer, and guidance. Our goal is to bring together women of all ages and stages for edification and service opportunities. As women grow and mature in godliness, they are better equipped to nurture and serve in their families, to enrich the church, and to evangelize their communities (Titus 2:3-6; 2 Tim. 2:2).

You must have a clear understanding of your church as well as your women and their needs to develop an effective women's ministry.

• The goal of women's enrichment ministry is to grow in our relationship with the Lord, to serve Him with our Christian sisters, and to minister to the world around us (1 Pet. 4:10).

Consider Childcare

If you intend to reach young mothers, you will need to consider how best to provide for their children during your women's ministry activities. If your church cannot cover the expense, consider charging a small fee (perhaps $1 per child) or passing the plate so all attending can help. Several youth, supervised by an adult, may volunteer their time or accept donations toward a youth camp or missions trip. You can ask for those who are not attending the function to volunteer their time to take care of the children. Often, grandmothers, due to distance from their families, are not able to spend much time with their grand-children. This may be the perfect ministry for them. For special women's events, the husbands may be willing to volunteer to provide extra help at no expense. If you provide a Bible lesson for the children during your weekly activities, moms will be even more encouraged to leave their children in childcare, knowing that their children's spiritual lives are also important to women's enrichment ministry. Remember to continually lift your childcare workers to the Father in prayer. They are a vital part of your ministry to women.

Determine Financial Needs

Consider your financial resources for your women's enrichment ministry. Is there budget money available to support this ministry? If not, you must make each endeavor recover its costs by selling tickets, charging for Bible study materials and child care, or taking donations. Remember to also consider the human resources available. There are many persons who would be happy to donate time and talents to help promote ministry for women.

Conduct a Survey

Compile and print the survey your survey study team has decided on. The most successful way to receive feedback from the survey is to promote it through Sunday morning Bible study. With the approval of your minister of education, take a few minutes at the beginning of the class or department time to explain why you are requesting that they complete the survey. Ask them to fill it out and hand it to you before their class begins. You may want to do this two Sundays in a row to allow participation of a greater number of women.

If you choose not to conduct a survey, there are other options for discovering needs. You can go to an uninvolved person or group and ask them what it would take to get them involved in ministry with women. You could also target a particular group such as young mothers or professional women and spend time talking with them to discover their needs. The goal is to uncover unmet needs and begin finding ways to meet those needs.

Organize Leadership

Once the survey is taken and the information compiled, it is time to choose a team leader, director, chairperson, coordinator, or other title you choose. This must be a woman who is an organizer, is diplomatic, has a faithful daily walk with Christ, and has time to devote to this ministry. Decide ahead of time how many studies or ministries you will offer, and add leaders for each area (see Building Your Leadership Team, page 60). Remember, you cannot do everything the first year. Use the results from the survey to determine what you will do first. Other opportunities may be added as needed to provide for growth of the ministry and the individuals in the ministry.

There are a number of organizational models in local churches. We have illustrated four at the end of this book (see pages 126-127). No two women's enrichment ministries will look alike. Get ideas from a variety of sources, but let God design a ministry unique to your church.

Communicate with the Church

As you promote your women's enrichment ministry, use a variety of ways to communicate to your church. Bulletin boards, church newsletters and bulletins, pulpit announcements, and mailings are excellent ways of getting the word out. (See "Publicity and Promotion," page 116.) Word of mouth may still be the most effective way of encouraging women to participate, grow, and minister. Challenge your women to invite at least two other women to your first event.

Kick Off Your Women's Enrichment Ministry

Make the kick-off for your new ministry special. You might plan a tea and time of fellowship and information to take place in a home. Your pastor's wife might want to be the hostess for this event. In each room of the home you could station one ministry leader. As women visit that room, they could learn about that area of ministry being offered as a part of the new women's enrichment ministry program for the year. A handout or favor including pertinent information would be beneficial. Allow time for leaders and participants to enjoy and get to know one another. Make sure each woman understands how special she is and what a benefit she would receive by being a part of your women's enrichment ministry. Help her see that there will be opportunities for her to grow and develop her spiritual life, develop relationships, share her faith, and minister to others. Let her know that your ministry needs her gifts and talents, also.

Study God's Word

Just as prayer must undergird women's enrichment ministry and is essential to its effectiveness, studying God's Word is also essential. Women must study the Bible diligently as they seek God's will for every area of their lives.

Bible study needs to be at the heart of your women's enrichment ministry. Plan various opportunities for your women. There are two in-depth Bible studies for women available from LifeWay Press.

• *A Woman's Heart, God's Dwelling Place* is an 11-week study of the Old Testament tabernacle. Author Beth Moore invites women to discover how God initiated a deeper relationship with His chosen people. By establishing His place of dwelling in the wilderness, God brought reconciliation, revealed His glory, and prefigured the coming of the true Tabernacle, Jesus Christ. Beth shows women how to take these biblical truths and apply them to their daily lives.

• *A Heart Like His: Seeking the Heart of God Through the Life of David* is about King David. The study helps women learn how they can have a heart after God's; what their potential is as a believer in Christ based on David's example—both for the divine and the disasters; what the specific warning signals are for temptation and sin; how they can accept God's forgiveness and return to the path of righteousness; and how God can be a part of the intricate relationships in their lives.

Any of the LIFE (Lay Institute for Equipping) courses such as *Experiencing God: Knowing and Doing the Will of God; The Mind of Christ; Heaven, Your Real Home, Life in the Spirit, First Place; Witnessing Through Your Relationships;* and *WiseCounsel: Skills for Lay Counseling* would be excellent study options for women's enrichment ministry participants. Six-week courses available are *In God's Presence: Your Daily Guide to a Meaningful Prayer Life, When God Speaks: How to Recognize God's Voice and Respond in Obedience,* and *Living God's Word: Practical Lessons for Applying Scripture to Life.* Support group resources such as *Making Peace with Your Past, Conquering Codependency,* and *Search for Significance* are also excellent tools to be used in your ministry.

Evaluate

Continual evaluation will keep your ministry fresh. Evaluate the effectiveness of studies, groups, leaders, projects, special events, and mission and service opportunities. By updating the program from year to year, you stay abreast of the current needs and how to meet those needs. (See sample evaluations on pages 44 and 45.)

Keep in mind as you further develop your women's enrichment ministry that to minister to women with various needs, you must offer a diverse ministry. As the needs of your women and their families change, your ministry options should change to meet those needs. Flexibility is a key to providing meaningful, effective ministry to and with women in your church and community.

Balance

Although the extent of ministries you can provide and the organizational structure may differ, the principals are the same whether you are a member of a large or small church. The key is balance. This is true in your own life as you balance what you take in spiritually with what you give back in service. There must also be balance in your women's enrichment ministry. One of my staff ministers once said, "Consumption without contribution makes for a stuffed Christian and contribution without consumption makes for a shallow Christian." We must offer options that provide spiritual, mental, emotional, relational, and physical growth. At the same time we must be continually encouraging those women to take what they are learning, put it into practice in their lives, and serve the Lord by reaching women for Christ and leading them to become disciples. Continue to pray and see where God is working, then boldly follow where He leads you and your leadership team as you help pass the baton of faith from generation to generation.

The key to an effective women's enrichment ministry is balance.

Leadership Evaluation

Help your large-group leader and small-group facilitator prepare for future leadership roles by evaluating their effectiveness in the following leadership areas.

Large-group Leader

Rank the following by number: (1) Excellent; (2) Good; (3) Fair; or (4) Needs improvement.

_____ Promoted the study adequately

_____ Conducted registration smoothly

_____ Had sufficient supplies available, (member books, pencils, Bibles)

_____ Arranged for comfortable and adequate meeting facilities

_____ Provided administrative leadership and organizational direction in a caring, efficient manner

_____ Clearly communicated logistical details and course requirements

_____ Conducted meaningful large-group sessions

_____ Handled problems effectively

Additional comments:

_____

_____

Small-group Facilitator

Rank the following by number: (1) Excellent; (2) Good; (3) Fair; or (4) Needs improvement.

_____ Began and ended sessions on time

_____ Was prepared

_____ Encouraged participation

_____ Created an atmosphere of love, concern, support, and acceptance

_____ Demonstrated sensitivity to the Holy Spirit's leadership

_____ Exhibited enthusiasm for the course and for God's Word

_____ Kept the focus on God's Word and His work in our lives

_____ Directed the discussion appropriately and meaningfully

_____ Was flexible in adapting the discussion questions according to the group's needs and interests

_____ Encouraged prayer for one another

_____ Worked to build relationships

_____ Handled problems effectively

Additional comments:

_____

_____

Program Evaluation

Please help us continue to provide an effective women's enrichment ministry by completing the following questionnaire.

1. Which activities did you participate in this period?

_____

_____

_____

2. What is your overall evaluation?
   ☐ What I expected
   ☐ Better than what I expected
   ☐ Less than what I expected

3. Which activities will you participate in next period?

_____

_____

4. What other topics or speakers would you like to have in our ministry?

_____

_____

5. Were there any problems we need to be aware of?   ☐ yes   ☐ no
If yes, please explain.

_____

_____

6. How can we best help you through our women's enrichment ministry?

_____

_____

(This evaluation may be used at the end of each period of women's enrichment ministry activities to help plan for the next year.)

Survey/Questionnaire

Please fill this out as completely as possible to help our church plan for women. Your responses are not binding. Check as many as apply to you.

1. Fellowship
I would participate in:

☐ Women's retreat (Friday night/Saturday) ☐ Prayer/share partners
☐ After-church fellowship ☐ New member activities
☐ Women's conference at the church ☐ Banquets and luncheons
☐ Other:_____

2. Study Opportunities
I would participate in:

☐ Discipleship studies
☐ Identifying spiritual gifts for ministry
☐ Women's Bible study
   ☐ Weekday   ☐ Weekday noon
   ☐ Weekday evening   ☐ Sunday evening
☐ Book reviews (Type: _____)
☐ Study of social and moral issues in our society
☐ Study of how to help others with personal problems (lay counseling)
☐ Study of prayer
☐ Other:_____

3. Missions/Evangelism
I would participate in:

☐ Witnessing training
☐ Praying for missionaries
☐ Short-term mission trip ☐ USA ☐ Overseas
☐ Interaction with local missionaries
☐ Other:_____

4. Community Ministries
If you speak a second language, please specify: _____
I would be willing to help our church expand its ministry in:

☐ Literacy   ☐ Medical/dentistry
☐ Tutoring   ☐ Homebound
☐ Children's home   ☐ Hospital ministry
☐ Prisons/jails/youth offenders   ☐ Internationals
☐ Campus ministry   ☐ Latch-key kids/hotline
☐ Handicapped/disabled persons   ☐ Meals-on-Wheels
☐ Clothes closet   ☐ Nursing homes/adopted grand-
☐ Soup kitchen/food closet   parents/aging
☐ Other:_____

5. Interests

I would participate in and/or teach:

Participate		Teach	Participate		Teach
☐	Calligraphy	☐	☐	Cooking/nutrition	☐
☐	Marriage enrichment	☐	☐	Creative writing	☐
☐	Drama	☐	☐	Car repair	☐
☐	Exercise	☐	☐	Financial planning	☐
☐	Gardening	☐	☐	First aid (with CPR)	☐
☐	Home repair	☐	☐	Interior decorating	☐
☐	Needlework	☐	☐	Quilting	☐
☐	Painting	☐	☐	Sewing	☐
☐	Ceramics	☐	☐	Parenting/grandparenting	☐
☐	Personal grooming	☐	☐	Self defense	☐
☐	Time management	☐	☐	Single again	☐
☐	Divorce recovery	☐	☐	Other:_____	☐

6. Talents

I would be willing to utilize my talents through:

☐	Artwork	☐	Nursery volunteers
☐	Distribution of information	☐	Bulletin boards
☐	Book reviews	☐	Photography
☐	Creative displays	☐	Telephoning
☐	Posters	☐	Creative writing
☐	Graphics	☐	Newsletters
☐	My speciality: _____		

7. Especially for Career Women

I would participate in and/or teach:

Participate		Teach
☐	Witnessing at work	☐
☐	Midlife careers	☐
☐	Christian ethics on the job	☐
☐	Beginning a business at home	☐
☐	Time management at home/work	☐
☐	The working mother and her relationship to her children	☐

8. Teaching/Leading

I am interested in teaching or leading:

☐	Bible Study	☐	*MasterLife*
☐	Music	☐	*A Woman's Heart*
☐	Vacation Bible School	☐	*Experiencing God*
☐	Sunday School	☐	*A Heart Like His*
☐	Retreats/conferences	☐	*The Mind of Christ*
☐	Preschoolers	☐	*Heaven … Your Real Home*
☐	Youth	☐	*WiseCounsel*
☐	Children	☐	*Disciple's Prayer Life*

(List continues on next page)

☐ Camps   ☐ Intercessory Prayer Ministry
☐ Median Adults   ☐ Young Adults
☐ Senior Adults   ☐ Other:_____

9. Speakers/Musicians

I would like to hear …
    ☐ Within our church membership_____
    ☐ Outside our church membership _____

Comments to improve or broaden women's enrichment ministry:

_____

_____

_____

10. Schedule

Daytime
    ☐ I could attend a weekly program. Best day: _____
    ☐ I could only attend a monthly meeting. Best time: _____
    ☐ I could only attend special events and projects periodically.

Nighttime
    ☐ I could attend a weekly program. Best night: _____
    ☐ I could only attend a monthly meeting. Best time: _____
    ☐ I could only attend special events and projects periodically.

11. Personal Profile

Age group
    ☐ 18-24   ☐ 25-32   ☐ 33-41
    ☐ 42-52   ☐ 53-62   ☐ 63-70   ☐ 71+

Status
    ☐ Single   ☐ Married   ☐ Widowed   ☐ Divorced

Ages of children at home, if any: _____

Employment
    ☐ Full-time homemaker   ☐ Employed outside the home part-time
    ☐ Home-based business   ☐ Employed outside the home full-time

I currently attend …
    ☐ Sunday School   ☐ Discipleship classes
    ☐ Women's Bible study   ☐ Women's retreats
    ☐ Women's conferences   ☐ Other:_____
    ☐ Mission's meetings/events

Were you active in women's enrichment ministries this past year?
☐ Yes ☐ No   Why or why not?

_____

_____

Have you ever been active in other women's groups? ☐ Yes ☐ No
Which groups?
  ☐ Bible Study Fellowship
  ☐ Precept Bible Study
  ☐ Christian Women's Club
  ☐ Other:_____

Name: _____

Address: _____

City/State/Zip: _____

Telephone: Home: _____

        Work: _____

Thank you for taking the time to complete this questionnaire.

Balanced Ministry

Monte McMahan Clendinning

Consider what the following have in common:

- a lovely flower arrangement;

- a lady's attractive outfit;

- an appealing living room;

- a well-proportioned, healthy body.

The word *balance* no doubt comes to mind. A lovely flower arrangement reveals symmetry and balance. Balance is achieved in a lady's attractively coordinated outfit through carefully selected color, texture, and style. An appealing room happens when all elements are in harmony. One primary factor necessary in producing a well-proportioned body is a well-balanced diet.

Balance can be defined as a steadiness resulting from all parts being properly adjusted to each other, with no one part outweighing or out of proportion to another.

In the same manner, an effective women's enrichment ministry is the result of balance. Such balance does not happen by chance or by wishing it to be so. Rather, it is the result of careful, prayerful planning. Women's leaders have the awesome responsibility of joining hands with God in helping women of their church become mature in Him. These leaders should never forget they are working with God's creation: "So God created man in His own image, in the image of God he created him; male and female he created them" (Gen. 1:27).

With a sense of awe, the psalmist joins other writers in the Old Testament in praising God:

For you created my inmost being;
    you knit me together in my mother's womb.
I praise you because I am fearfully and wonderfully made (Ps. 139:13-14).

Women are special because God created them! He made provision for their salvation through Jesus. Every woman in the church is special, whether she is the most inactive church member or the most prominent leader. Each is gifted by God and has a special contribution to make in building up the body of Christ. Women's enrichment ministries seek to involve women in such a way that all might grow toward maturity in Christ and find their places in extending God's kingdom.

The leader of the women's enrichment ministry in the local church will find help in developing women by asking questions such as:

1. What is our purpose, or reason for being?

2. What are some general observations to be considered in developing a women's ministry?

3. What are the basic elements necessary to develop a well-balanced women's ministry?

4. How is balance maintained?

This chapter seeks to address each of these questions.

A significant component to remember is *time*. Flowers, outfits, rooms, bodies, and a well-balanced women's ministry do not happen overnight. Maturity and growth—both physical and spiritual—develop over a period of time. The final product is not completed all at once. While all factors may not be developed simultaneously, the ultimate goal is balance for the total program. Leaders should keep in mind this goal as they give attention to a proper balance of factors throughout the process of growth.

Relating Purpose and Balance

Examine the purpose statement of your women's enrichment ministry to discover its intent, its scope, and how it relates to your church's mission or vision statement. If such a statement has not been recorded, encourage women's leaders representing all phases of church life to work along with a church staff member to write one. They will want to spend time in God's Word and in prayer as they seek to develop this foundational statement which reflects the direction and spirit of the mission or vision statement of the church itself. In addition, they will consider the functions of a church, evangelism, discipleship, ministry, fellowship, and worship.[1] In this particular grouping, missions is listed as a result of evangelism. Women's enrichment ministry is not separate from the church; it helps the church accomplish its God-given mission.

In following this process, the women of Travis Avenue Baptist Church in Fort Worth, Texas penned this purpose statement: *Our purpose is to equip our women toward maturity in Christ; fellowship with one another; service through our church; sharing Jesus with family, friends and others; and involvement in missions locally and around the world.*

Four key ideas from their statement guide the choice of curriculum.

1. Maturity in Christ immediately brings to mind the need for Bible and discipleship studies which contribute to each woman's spiritual growth, thus, in turn, touching her family.

2. Fellowship with one another calls for an understanding of how Christians should relate to each other.

3. Service through the church should give a woman the opportunity to identify and use her spiritual gift(s) in ministry to meet needs of individuals in her church and community.

Women's enrichment ministry helps the church accomplish its God-given mission.

4. Sharing Christ grows out of a woman's personal experience with Jesus and being equipped to share her faith.

5. Involvement in missions through study, prayer, giving money, and short- or long-term missions reminds women that missions is not optional.

A purpose statement not only aids in developing a balanced ministry for the women of the church but serves as a tool for evaluation. Giving proper attention to a purpose statement in light of the church's functions and mission/vision statement can contribute to a larger vision for women's enrichment ministries than if women develop their own activities without giving consideration to fitting into the church's mission. Women are wise to plan for the years—not just for the year. What an awesome responsibility leaders carry! They seek God's vision for what a woman should be in 10 or 20 years and are busily engaged in offering curriculum which can be used of God to help that woman toward maturing in Him.

Michelangelo, the famous Italian sculptor, had a vision for each of his sculptures. Biographers report that he could look at a piece of marble and envision a form to be released from that block of marble. Just so, women's leaders need God's vision of what women can become, and need to be ready to create classes and activities in which they might mature in Christ.

Women's enrichment ministries in all churches do not have to look alike. Just as God has made each woman different, work among women will differ from church to church. Regardless of form, the elements should be the same to ensure a balanced ministry.

Developing a Balanced Ministry

Before addressing specific topics to be included in women's enrichment ministry, let me make three general observations.

General Context and Balance

Leaders should reflect on the context in which the balance is to be achieved in their local church and denomination. A careful listing of what the local church offers women through different settings will help avoid duplications. Consider where women are involved in the life of the church. Create new classes and activities only where needed. If meaningful classes and experiences already exist, take advantage of networking with them.

For example, in Sunday night discipleship a church might offer *Experiencing God*. A group of women who wish to take a personal growth class cannot be present on Sunday night, but could attend a weekday class. Instead of developing something different, why not offer *Experiencing God* on a weekday when those women can attend? One of the teachers who has already prepared for the Sunday night sessions might be available to lead the group during the week.

A look at your denomination may reveal a strong emphasis on Bible study, evangelism, and missions. What is being done in your women's enrichment ministry to involve women in Bible study, evangelism, and missions?

While Bible study is basic throughout the Sunday School, there seems to be a hunger in the hearts of women today for a deeper understanding of God's Word. Therefore, most women's enrichment ministries offer Bible study for a large group, or small groups, or in different settings.

Women's enrichment ministries in all churches do not have to look alike.

Are the women of the church equipped to share their faith effectively? Do they know how to share Christ with others, beginning with their own family members? Many may have taken advantage of special training sessions such as CWT (Christian Witnessing Training). (For more information on witnessing resources, see page 124.) However, large numbers of women have not developed a lifestyle of witnessing. This should become a serious study and practice in women's enrichment ministries.

Closely related to evangelism is missions. Some women's enrichment ministries have overlooked the priority of missions for women's involvement. If a women's organization such as Women on Mission is already in place in the church, networking with that organization can take advantage of that expertise. If not, develop missions involvement for your women. Missions and evangelism both need to be incorporated into a woman's lifestyle. Neither is optional. Both are commanded by Jesus Himself, "But you will receive power when the Holy Spirit comes on you; and you will be my witnesses in Jerusalem, and in all Judea and Samaria, and to the ends of the earth" (Acts 1:8).

Leaders need to be open to God's work among women and draw ideas from all kinds of effective ministries. Their ultimate responsibility is to develop classes and programs to serve women in their church and denomination.

Women's Needs Versus Desires

A helpful guiding question throughout developing a women's enrichment ministry is "What does Jesus want the women of my church to become?" While most women's leaders would agree that this is significant, in practice this is sometimes forgotten in the eagerness to offer growth opportunities suggested by the women themselves. Tension may develop in the minds of those who design women's enrichment ministries between what women say they want and what Jesus indicates they need. A balanced ministry will offer both subjects women want and subjects necessary for Christian discipline and growth. Again, keeping a balance is important. For example, consider Jan's experience.

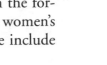

"What does Jesus want the women of my church to become?"

Jan (a fictitious name) was attracted to a church's women's enrichment ministry through a craft class being offered after the Bible study. Although she was a Christian, she had no interest in Bible study, and came only in time for the craft class. A friend asked her to attend the Bible study with her. Finally Jan agreed to go, but only to please the friend and to be on time for craft class.

Little by little Jan became interested in the Bible study as she came to realize God's truths were relevant to her needs today. Much to her surprise, she found herself looking forward to each week's Bible study as well as to the craft class.

Several years later, Jan moved to another state. She wrote a friend in the former church, "Can you believe it? The women in my church had no women's enrichment ministry, so I helped them pull one together. And, yes, we include both crafts and Bible study!"

Had that original women's enrichment ministry been organized only on what women such as Jan desired, they would have missed their opportunity to help women become better grounded in God's Word. "Sanctified bait" is the label one woman placed on classes such as crafts. She believes God can use even those kinds of personal interest groups to draw women toward a greater interest in spiritual matters.

Balancing the New and the Old

Reference was made earlier to a well-dressed woman and the place balance has in her wardrobe. A closer look at what she is wearing might reveal a stunning piece of jewelry which belonged to her grandmother. Rather than discarding an old piece, such a piece mounted in a new setting actually enhances it.

And in a pleasantly decorated home a woman often points with pride to furniture which came from her family of origin. She knows that old piece of furniture in the proper setting lends charm and a sense of stability to the room, furnishing a significant link to the past.

And what do these ideas have to do with women's enrichment ministries? Many churches have an organization called Women on Mission. Women who have not been recently involved with this organization may be totally unaware of the significant changes. Today's woman would do well to become a part of the heartbeat of a movement which has helped women for over a century reach out and minister to peoples of the world — for Jesus' sake.

Balance the old and the new. When the old is discarded altogether, the new can never have the depth, beauty, and balance it could have when God's balance is achieved between the old and the new. In the same manner, if the "old" maintains its original ways without sensitivity to needed changes, it can hinder a freshness of God's Spirit in permeating the group.

Basic Elements for a Balanced Ministry

The Person (Woman Learner)

Three factors are present in every woman: mind, heart, and will.

Women may differ in appearance, temperament, and spiritual growth; but three factors are present in every woman: mind, heart, and will. Women think; they are emotional; and they are doers. While some have a tendency toward one more than another, all three are important parts of the woman learner and must be involved to complete the learning cycle. Christian educators quickly point out the significance of the Holy Spirit as the teacher (see John 14:26). Leaders unaware of these three elements could actually interfere with the balanced growth of women. For instance, the program that offers study opportunities alone could not adequately qualify for the completed learning cycle.

Mind

A woman's mind must be involved if she is to learn and grow. She needs to read, study, think, memorize, and reason. As significant as this is, learning is incomplete if the heart and will do not follow.

Heart

It seems God has given women an unusual capacity to feel. When a woman studies something, her heart needs to be involved. She should ask herself such questions as: "What does this truth mean to me?" "How do I feel about it?" "How does it touch me?" Without the heart, learning can be intellectual and cold. The use of the heart in applying the truth helps personalize the truth. But again, if women's enrichment ministries are planned to reach the heart only—apart from the mind and will—there is an imbalance in learning.

Will

The third factor is the will. The woman learner must know the truth; feel the truth; but now she asks the question: "What will I do with this truth?" Or, "Because I have read a certain truth and responded to it from my heart, what action will I pursue?" Perhaps an example will help explain this concept.

Suppose a devastating tornado strikes the area of town where you live. A woman reads about it in the newspaper (mind). As she reflects on the destruction, she feels for the people involved who have lost their homes and all they have (heart) and begins to ponder what she could do to help. As she seeks God's guidance as to how she can help, she decides (will) to gather up extra clothing, bedding, and food and take them to victims of the vicious tornado. Thus, a woman's mind, heart, and will all are involved in this learning situation.

In developing a well-balanced women's enrichment ministry, careful attention should be given to planning opportunities in which women can keep a balance in their lives between study and service. The woman who devotes her energies only to service without replenishing her spirit may face burnout. Likewise, the woman who only studies without serving will not grow as she could.

Jesus is the model. Numerous accounts in the Gospels refer to His taking time to be alone with God. Others reveal His compassionate heart. And Mark 10:45 reveals His servant heart, "For even the Son of Man did not come to be served, but to serve, and to give his life as a ransom for many."

The Process (How Women Learn)

As we discussed the person, we introduced the process of learning. We established the necessity for the mind, heart, and will to be involved for complete and balanced learning to occur. Learning deals with such questions as:

1. What courses and other learning experiences could I offer women of our church to involve the use of their minds, hearts, and wills?

2. When we involve the minds of women, what level of learning do we want them to reach? For example, do we want them to learn statements and facts alone, or to understand what they study, or to be able to apply truths—or even higher forms in the scale of what educators call cognitive (intellectual) learning?

Dr. William "Budd" Smith refers to Benjamin S. Bloom's definition of cognitive learning which deals "with the recall or recognition of knowledge and the development of intellectual abilities and skills."[2] In the same manner he recognizes affective (emotional) learning as "objectives which describe changes in interest, attitudes, and values, and the development of appreciations and adequate adjustment."[3] Those changes, of course, are to be voluntary.

Do women's leaders wish to involve learners in such a way as to enhance their value systems? In cooperation with the Holy Spirit, are the activities in women's enrichment ministries designed to lead each woman to a total commitment to Jesus Christ which is consistently reflected in her lifestyle?

Women's enrichment ministry leaders have the awesome responsibility of joining hands with God to select courses, teachers, and activities to lead women to that total commitment to the Christian lifestyle. Much prayer and thought must be invested in designing a women's enrichment ministry to ensure the desired well-balanced program.

If you desire to explore more deeply the learning process, read *The Teaching Ministry of the Church*, written by six seminary professors immersed in the field of teaching and foundations.

Probing the subject of how a person learns should not dishearten the leader, but rather challenge her to offer the very best opportunities available to help women mature in Christ.

The Plan (Curriculum)

In one sense curriculum is the sum total of a person's life experiences—intellect, emotions, and actions. Webster defines curriculum as "a set of courses constituting an area of specialization."

The Women's Enrichment Ministry Wheel can give direction to the desired balanced development.

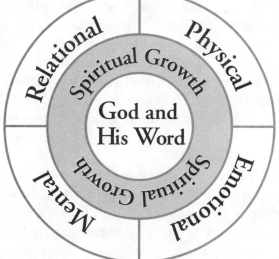

A look at the various components will give assistance in the search for balance in a women's enrichment ministry.

God and His Word

At the center of the wheel is God's Word. Notice the wording, "God and His Word." Not only does this suggest that Bible study is central and basic for women's enrichment ministries, but the emphasis is on a personal relationship with God through Jesus. The goal is for every woman to know Jesus as personal Savior. Growth cannot occur until there is birth.

Spiritual Growth

This concentric circle surrounds "God and His Word" and is an outgrowth of the center. After a woman becomes a Christian, she is nurtured through God's Word toward maturity in Christ. This includes application of God's Word, prayer, and discipleship. Four large areas of growth make up the next circle.

Relational Growth

Relational growth includes family issues; fellowshipping with Christians and others; communicating effectively; sharing your faith in Jesus Christ and developing a missions lifestyle; and being involved in ministry through the church.

A woman's spiritual growth should include a deeper understanding of how to love unconditionally—like Jesus. This kind of revolutionary love is called agape. One of Jesus' last commands is "A new command I give you: Love one another. As I have loved you, so you must love one another" (John 13:34). Women who love as Jesus did—accepting, forgiving, building up, taking the initiative—are learning how to love unconditionally.

Physical growth

"Do you not know that your body is a temple of the Holy Spirit, who is in you, whom you have received from God?" (1 Cor. 6:19). Such knowledge should prompt women to carefully consider taking good care of their bodies. Therefore, attention should be given to a woman's health, nutrition, and, where necessary, addictions. Some churches offer excellent programs in this area. Therefore, networking may be all that is necessary. If these programs are not available, women should be provided opportunities to participate in them. Consider the human and financial resources in your church and provide classes for your women.

Emotional growth

Thought should be given to how to help women with self-esteem problems, depression, crises, and counseling needs. In New Testament times Jesus raised the status of women to unbelievable heights. Prior to that time they had been bartered. As women grow in Christ, they should be learning who they are in Christ — valued, loved people.

Mental growth

Women should be acquiring skills to help them toward maturity. Therefore, women's enrichment ministries should consider offering help in decision-making, time management, stress management, finances, and leadership. Women need to be open to acquiring an enlarged vision of the world, determined to find their places in God's purpose for the world.

The Women's Enrichment Ministry Wheel along with a purpose statement, can help develop a well-balanced women's enrichment ministry. If a leader haphazardly selects courses, more than likely haphazard growth will occur. She might plan electives and overlook basics for spiritual development. Or, she might plan only basics and hinder the growth of women by not including electives. Basics upon which electives might be built will lend themselves to balanced ministries.

The Power (Spiritual)

The spiritual element of a balanced ministry is God's work, and God has the power available to accomplish all He wants to accomplish. An amazing thought is that God chooses to use human instruments through which His power and love can flow. God reminded King Jehoshaphat, "Do not be afraid or discouraged. … The battle is not yours, but God's" (2 Chron. 20:15).

While many ministries provide a women's prayer group, they often do not plan a strategy of prayer to undergird women's enrichment ministry. One of the best ways to ensure balance is through concerted prayer from such a strategy.

One approach might be organizing a prayer network for the sole purpose of undergirding the ministries in which women are involved. Personal prayer requests, except in case of emergencies, should not be included. Rather, the chairperson or a designated woman could elicit priority prayer requests from each leader of women's work. Include prayer for major events of the church.

Consider including a representative from every phase of women's work in the church. An effective balance could be achieved when an attempt is made to include women of different ages—chronological and spiritual. This group would meet on a regular schedule, lifting to the Father requests from the previously prepared list. When appropriate, thanksgiving can be offered for answered prayers. Each group member should leave with at least one prayer request for which she will pray for a specified length of time. Where tried, this plan has had amazing results. An added benefit has been the bonding of group members.

A word of caution: a women's enrichment ministry cannot meet all needs of women. It can help identify needs and offer suggestions of where women might find help in meeting those needs. The women's enrichment ministry is one part of the entire church. Some of those needs may be met through participation in established programs outside the parameters of the women's enrichment ministry. Cooperation and networking need to be present as women's enrichment ministry leaders help women develop toward full maturity in Christ.

Maintaining a Balanced Ministry

A balanced ministry can be maintained through regular evaluation, sensitive observation, and an outsider's perspective. Let's look at each of these.

Regular Evaluation

How can a leader know when she has an effective balance in her women's enrichment ministry? Leaders should evaluate their ministries on a regular basis. Every 12 months offers a good time for analyzing. A purpose statement created and adopted by the women can be a helpful tool. For example, one group identified fellowship as an important part of their ministry. Their format included a Bible study for all ages of women. In evaluating this particular phase of their ministry, leaders observed the interaction among the different ages and how they ministered to one another when special needs arose. They also took note of reactions from visitors in the meetings. One out-of-town visitor remarked, "I am amazed at the large number of women of different ages gathered together for Bible study—and they all seem to have a great time just being together!"

Each phase of your ministry should be evaluated. Check your ministry against the purpose statement and/or elements in the Women's Enrichment Ministry Wheel. Where there are successes, thank God and celebrate. Identify the area (or areas) where progress is needed; try to determine why that particular area has not progressed. Talk with the leaders involved. Prayerfully seek

Remember that your women's enrichment ministry is one part of the entire church.

God's direction for improving. Always be alert to enlarging your women's enrichment ministry to include new church members or those who have acquired a new status. For example, new retirees may now be available.

Sensitive Observation

Consider the spirit among the women. Do they have a spirit of anticipation, excitement, and joy? Observing statistics can be helpful, such as the number enrolled and attending in each group or activity. Since women are "feelers," observe the level of enthusiasm with which they participate.

Look for changes in the lives of women. Are the women achieving a better balance in their personal lives as they grow more like Jesus?

An Outsider's Perspective

An outsider's perspective offers an objective view of your ministry. Your church staff is a great resource. For example, ask your pastor for his impression of your women's enrichment ministry. When one women's enrichment ministry group asked their pastor to share his evaluation of their ministries, he replied,

"The women's enrichment ministry of our church is an integral part of our ministries. I find several strengths:

1. It is balanced. There is an excellent blend of evangelism and missions, the fun and the serious, the young and the old, self-improvement and service to others.

2. It is biblical. At the heart of our program is our women's encounter with the Word of God.

3. It is supportive. Our women's enrichment ministry leadership want the ministry to fit squarely into the overarching goals of our church.

As a pastor, I cannot imagine our church functioning effectively without our ministry to and with women."

Conclusion

Just as balance is needed in various physical aspects of a woman's life, so is balance needed in women's enrichment ministry to assist women in their desire to become what God created them to be.

Do not be discouraged if you cannot develop a full-blown, well-balanced women's enrichment ministry at the very outset. Develop what you can, making sure that the courses and activities are a valid part of the master plan. Keep on keeping on. Each year focus on additional activities which will help you come closer to your goal of balance. Keep your eyes on Jesus, who is "the author and perfecter of our faith" (Hebrews 12:2). You are a significant link between God and the precious women with whom you travel toward maturity in Christ. What a responsibility! What a privilege!

"Honest scales and balances are from the Lord;

all the weights in the bag are of his making" (Prov. 16:11).

---

[1] Gene Mims, *Kingdom Principles for Church Growth* (Nashville: Convention Press, 1994), 34.

[2] Benjamin S. Bloom, ed., *Taxonomy of Educational Objectives: Handbook I* (New York: David McKay Company, 1956), as quoted by Daryl Eldridge, ed., *The Teaching Ministry of the Church* (Nashville: Broadman and Holman Publishers, 1995), 270.

[3] Ibid., 271.

Building Your Leadership Team

Chris Adams

As you were growing up, who did you follow? Who were your heroes? Whoever they were, thcy were your leaders. If you look back, would you follow the same leaders today? Do you think of yourself as a leader? What are you doing to build a team of godly leaders that others will desire to follow because of their commitment to Christ?

This chapter will help you build that kind of team in your women's enrichment ministry as you encourage women to respond to God's call to leadership. All Christians are called to be leaders in one way or another. One of the privileges of being a women's enrichment ministry leader is helping women discover their giftedness and leadership abilities, and matching those with ministry opportunities.

Since Satan often attacks spiritual leaders first, we must pray to discover God's direction before beginning a new ministry or seeking leadership for that ministry. We then need to continue in prayer for those leaders as they serve. Sometimes we are tempted to begin a new ministry that the Lord has laid on our hearts, but there seems to be no leader. Waiting for God to raise up the right person is sometimes difficult, but the results will come from His plan and will be much more effective than if we rush into a new ministry on our own.

As a leader, you must place high priority on your own spiritual preparation. Are you spending time daily alone with God in prayer, worship, and Bible study? Those you lead must be able to see your walk with the Lord and your desire to continue to grow spiritually. If you are not setting the example, those you lead may not see the importance of a continual daily walk that draws women into a closer relationship with Christ.

Defining Leadership

Is leadership something you accomplish or acquire? Neither, it is a gift from the Heavenly Father. Leadership is the ability to influence people toward a common goal. In women's enrichment ministry, it is sharing the vision of reaching and discipling women for Christ.

Matthew 20:25-28 gives us quite a contrast between servant leadership and ruler leadership. "But Jesus called them to Himself and said, 'You know that the rulers of the Gentiles lord it over them, and those who are great exercise authority over them. Yet it shall not be so among you; but whoever desires to become great among you, let him be your servant. And whoever desires to be first among you, let him be your slave—just as the Son of Man did not come to be served, but to serve and to give His life a ransom for many" (NKJV). Rulers are "over" others. They exercise authority, tell others what to do, and coerce to get the results. Servants are "among" the others. They show and persuade in love. Servant leadership should be the goal for those in any position of leadership.

Rulers are "over" others; servants are "among" others.

Portrait of a Leader

We could use many words to describe a leader. Let's look at a few.

• *Enthusiastic*   She has an obvious passion for the Lord, for women, and for ministry to and with women.

• *Encouraging*   She will encourage others to lead and serve the Lord through various ministries, not just women's ministry.

• *Flexible*   She has learned how to make adjustments without allowing the situation to fall apart if things do not occur as expected.

• *Innovative*   She is not afraid to take risks if God has led her to step out of the "norm" and do some things that "have never been done before."

• *Available*   She allows God to direct her time and priorities to serve Him wholeheartedly.

• *Delegator*   She knows how to let go of control of the ministry and allow others to take responsibilities without watching over each detail. She allows leaders the freedom to be creative.

• *Listener*   She knows how to listen to those she leads so that she hears and understands their hearts. She affirms their contribution as important to the team.

• *Trainer*   She continues to learn so that she can train others as well as keep them informed of training opportunities offered by others.

• *Nurturer/Discipler*   She is as concerned about the spiritual growth of her team as she is in developing leadership skills.

• *Transparent*   She is transparent about her own failures and weaknesses so those she leads will be able to come to her when they struggle.

• *Accountable*   She allows and expects the Lord and her team to hold her accountable for her leadership and spiritual walk.

• *Evaluator*   She continually evaluates activities, studies, leaders, and ministries to make sure they are effective and current.

• *Dependable*   She will stand by her commitments to the best of her ability.

What does a leader look like? YOU! Unique and gifted to serve wherever God leads you. If God has called you to lead, He has equipped you to do all He asks.

"We are His workmanship, created in Christ Jesus for good works, which God prepared beforehand that we should walk in them" (Eph. 2:10, NKJV). God has already prepared beforehand all He wants us to do to serve Him. God's indwelling Holy Spirit provides the power to be obedient when He calls.

Mobilizing a Leadership Team

A Christian team could be described as a group of people who serve each other under Christ. In women's enrichment ministry, the team is made up of leaders who have responsibility for various aspects of the ministry to women in their church. Just as Jesus was a team leader and member, the women's enrichment ministry coordinator/director/team leader serves in both capacities. She works alongside her team, but also understands that the buck has to stop somewhere.

Because women are so busy today and sometimes hesitant to commit to many things, it is not easy to enlist leaders and volunteers to meet ministry needs. But it can be done and women will serve. The *Indiana Baptist* reported these reasons people say yes to volunteer opportunities:

"It sounds like fun.

I want to be where the action is.

They really need and want me.

It is a chance to learn new skills.

It could help me with my personal life.

I have gotten a lot of help; now it is my turn to repay.

It is a critical need; I have got to do my part.

I will have a chance to really influence what happens.

Service is a tradition in our family. It's expected.

My best friend is asking me.

I will make new friends."[1]

As we begin praying for leaders, it will be wise to consider these reasons.

Mobilizing a team is essential for effective ministry to women. Brad Smith says that a lay mobilization system works with existing church programs if it includes the following components: assimilation, context, discovery, matching, placement, coaching, and recognition.[2] Let's look closely at each one.

Assimilation means becoming a part of the church. As women join the church, we must be sure they find their niche, a place they can grow as well as serve. Providing a ministry for these women new to the church speeds up assimilation and makes sure new women do not get forgotten.

Context refers to helping women understand the biblical basis for volunteer service. Jesus commissioned His followers to go and make disciples of others (see Matt. 28:19-20). We must teach women that throughout Scripture we are instructed to share, go, serve, and witness.

Discovery of spiritual gifts and interests is an important part of developing women into leaders. We can encourage the use of spiritual gifts inventories and studies to help each woman discover how and why God has uniquely gifted her.

Matching shows women how to connect their gifts and interests with service opportunities.

Placement is selecting the best opportunity for service based on gifts and interests. This is much more effective than just filling an empty position.

Mobilizing a leadership team is essential for effective ministry to women.

Coaching should continue for each woman as she serves. As a team leader your responsibility is to offer training and encouragement.

Recognition happens as you offer times for celebration of service. This could be an appreciation service or banquet to say thank you for their willingness, sacrifice, and hard work.

Discovering Leaders

As you pray, there are several ways you may discover team members for specific assignments. Ask your pastor and other staff members for suggestions. They come in contact with many potential leaders and can point you to them. Other leaders in your church may also be able to provide suggestions.

Surveys can be helpful to discover talents, interests, and gifts needed for each area of service. If your church does not encourage surveys, discover leaders on your own by praying and watching women as you attend worship, Sunday morning Bible study, and other church activities.

A leadership team should be made up of women from different life stages and generations. This way you will get input from various groups like single and senior adult women, young moms, empty nesters, professionals, women sandwiched between aging parents and children at home, full-time homemakers, and so on. Remember that all these women will take the excitement of women's enrichment ministry and promote activities in their circles of influence.

Your team should also include different leadership styles. If you only choose women like yourself, there will not be balance in your planning or ministry. You need drivers who provide energy and excitement to complete the task at hand. Initiators enjoy beginning new ministries. Detailers will spend much time making sure all the bases have been covered. Listeners tend to listen quietly to all the discussion and then share an important conclusion. The innovator is not afraid to take risks.

Respect and value all leadership styles, gifts, knowledge, experience, and personalities. Including various styles of leaders will help ensure an effective team for ministry. Every woman has something to contribute. Help her find her passion and discover how to use it to serve Christ. Remember, God uses ordinary, inadequate people to accomplish extraordinary ministry through His power.

With all these different types of leaders, what should you look for? Look for *faithfulness* in their walk with the Lord. Are they growing spiritually? Are they spending time with Christ each day in prayer and Bible study? Look for *teachability.* Those leaders willing to listen and learn will continue to grow in service. Look for *availability.* Ministry takes time and willingness to be available.

Respect and value all leadership styles, gifts, experiences, and personalities.

Enlisting Leaders

In approaching these potential leaders, ask for a time when you can visit with them. You might even conduct an interview to discover any interest in the ministry. Define job expectations in detail. Always give time for them to pray and seek God's direction before responding to your request. Be supportive of their response whether or not they accept the leadership position being offered.

Mary Frances Bowley, First Baptist Church, Peachtree City, Georgia uses the following criteria for leadership.

1. Have a God-planted desire to be a member of this team. We want God to choose the team.
2. Display team building qualities.
   - Love Jesus.
   - Love people.
   - Know God's Word.
   - Know what authority is.
   - Be able to take responsibility.
3. Demonstrate a depth of commitment.
   - Participate in an in-depth Bible study.
   - Pray for the same 30 families (from Sunday School and church rolls) on a continuous basis (five per day six days a week); on the seventh day, pray for team members and their families.
   - Understand the vision God has given our church to use women's enrichment ministry as an outreach to our community and to strengthen the body of believers; communicate this to the women of our church.
   - Be willing to meet monthly for planning, fellowship, and prayer.

Training Leaders

Once you discover and enlist leaders to be on your leadership team, they need to be trained. The degree of training you provide will be reflected in the effectiveness of your women's enrichment ministry. Consider the following elements as you set up your training.

Prayer

The degree of training you provide your leaders will be reflected in the effectiveness of your ministry.

The most important area in training your leaders is prayer. This is the key to all you do in women's enrichment ministry; it even ranks above developing leader skills. Model the importance of prayer by beginning and concluding each meeting with prayer. Teach your leaders to be pray-ers, not just do-ers. Schedule times strictly for prayer and praise. Simply ask "What is God doing in your life?" These may be retreats lasting a few hours or overnight. Prayer will help avoid burnout among your team members and keep them focused on God's will for your ministry. Assign team members prayer partners for continued prayer for specific needs between planning meetings. Encourage your leaders to become involved in the intercessory prayer ministry of your church. Let your team know that you pray for them. Making prayer a priority will teach leaders to continually seek and respond to the Lord's guidance in all aspects of their lives, especially as they lead the women of your church and community.

Study

Studying *Experiencing God: Knowing and Doing the Will of God* as a group can also enhance and encourage spiritual growth among your team members. As you learn that ministry is what God does, not what we do, you begin to see where He is already at work. When God invites you to join Him in ministry, your team is ready and willing to obey His call.

Purpose and Vision

Keeping your ministry's purpose and vision in front of the team at all times will help focus the ministry. Check to make sure all plans will accomplish the purpose God has given the team. Many people die without Christ every day. Ask, "What will this activity or event do to reach women for Christ and disciple women in Christ?" If this is not going to be accomplished, maybe your plans need to be changed or replaced.

Ongoing Planning

To encourage and show accountability, there must be ongoing planning. This means not only meeting once or twice a year for strategic planning for the future, but also conducting monthly planning meetings to carry out the strategic plans. As you share important information with the team, allow for feedback from each person. What is happening in their area of ministry? Are there any special praises to share? What about problem areas? Are plans proceeding according to the schedule? Do adjustments need to be made? This is a time for team members to report to the rest of the team both their needs and joys.

Assistance

Each team member should always seek others to assist her with her area of ministry. The more people the team member involves, the greater the outcome of each event or activity. As committees and work groups share responsibilities, the circle of influence involves more women.

Teamwork is not hierarchy. As team leader, you may need to give specific instructions about an assigned task. But you should give ownership to those on your team by allowing decisions to be made at the lowest possible level. This empowers your leaders to make decisions about change, accomplish tasks, and validates their responsibilities. William Easum says, "Today's leaders focus on permission-giving rather than control or managing. They network individuals and teams through a shared vision of a preferred future. They facilitate ministry in others. They do not 'give' orders, or dictate how people must operate within the organization. They cast the vision that creates victory, that frees people to make on-the-spot decisions and then get out of the way. In this role they model an open and free environment in which ordinary people are encouraged and equipped to do extraordinary ministry. Their passion is to develop other leaders who will develop other leaders."[3]

Encouragement

As team leader, you are the head cheerleader for the team. Encourage your leaders often. Share with them Ephesians 2:10: "We are His workmanship, created in Christ Jesus for good works, which God prepared beforehand that we should walk in them." God will equip them for everything He calls them to do. Recognize their service–the job itself and what it took to do it. Send thank you notes to your leaders, and to their families for supporting them. Continue to remind them of your prayers for them, their area of service, and their families.

Encourage them to be innovative and to take risks. Remember, Jesus was pretty radical, too! If they experience failure in some aspect of their ministry, be

As team leader, you are the head cheerleader for the team.

there to help them regroup and carry on. We often learn more from failure than from success.

Learning Style
As you train your leaders, be aware of their different learning styles. Some learn best by listening to others talk in person, through radio, television, and audio tapes. Some learn best by reading books, newspapers, and magazines. Visual aids will enhance their learning. Others must have hands-on experience to learn best. Some can work alone without assistance. Discover what types of learners you have on your team, and check to see if your training includes all types of teaching so that each woman will learn according to her style.

Network
Always maintain contact with the network of people who provide leadership training on an associational, state, or national level. Take your team to the training events that will be most beneficial to them as individuals and team players.

Leadership Teams
There are many types of women's enrichment ministry leadership teams. Even though your core leaders may provide the foundation for the ministry and may serve for two or three years, you must also establish other types of leadership teams. Let's take a look at some of these teams and the benefit each one offers.

There are many types of women's enrichment ministry leadership teams.

- Coleaders: This approach offers two busy women the opportunity to join together to accomplish a task.
- Short-term: Short-term responsibilities mean there is closure at the end of a set time period (perhaps 4 to 12 weeks).
- Project: Committing to a single project means there is closure once the project has been completed.
- Ongoing: This team lays the foundation for the daily and weekly ministries. Leaders generally serve from one to three years.
- Dream Team: This may be called the assessment or think-tank team. These women provide the stimulus to continue to look to the future for growth, change, and ministry development. In "The Mindset of Today's Changing Woman," Denise Farrar says,

> There will be one striking characteristic of third generation Women's Ministries. They will incorporate a group into their ministry that could be called a 'think-tank group.' The purpose of this group will be to focus on emerging trends and patterns. Most women's organizations have some type of decision-making group, but their focus is on implementation and coordination. Ministries on the cutting edge will have a separate group focused on the current trends and patterns affecting women as well as their needs. ... These women need to be innovative, change-agent types of leaders.[4]

This team, made up of women from all seasons of life, may only meet once or twice a year.
- Leader/Learner: This team is made up of a leader and an apprentice. The leader mentors the understudy as she carries out her responsibilities. The one

learning is expected to take the leadership position after a specific time period when the leader steps down or into another area of service. William Easum says, "If you are able to see in people more than they can see in themselves and are willing to equip them and set them free, you have the ability to be a leader in the Quantum Age. Mentors always have interns or apprentices and they take the long term view instead of looking for the quick fixes."[5] These leaders are concerned about the future of the ministry and who will carry on after them.

Team Member Assignments

Following are some suggestions for team responsibilities. Use these as a beginning point as you design your ministry team to meet the needs of your church.

Director

The director is the administrator who:

• oversees planning, coordination, and implementation of all discipleship, outreach, evangelism, and fellowship activities, leaders, and volunteers for women's ministry;

• provides training and motivation for women's enrichment ministry leaders;

• prepares and sets the agenda for, as well as chairs, all planning meetings and retreats;

• prepares and oversees the annual budget and calendar; works closely with other church leaders.

Suggested Teams

The women's enrichment ministry director in consultation with the core leadership team will oversee all teams. The number and size of each team depends on the size of the church and extent of the women's enrichment ministry. You may not need all of these; you may want to combine some of them. Use only those that apply to your ministry. There will not be a need for all of them if the women's enrichment ministry is fairly new. The following teams may be composed of a group of women or one person.

Hospitality

Greets and makes each woman feel welcome at all women's activities.

Facilities

Makes sure proper procedures have been followed for securing buildings and rooms needed for each activity or event.

Program

Helps develop effective ministry through ongoing weekly studies and groups such as electives, personal choice studies, and Bible studies; previews each study; secures leaders for each group.

Child Care

Provides quality childcare and learning opportunities for children while their mothers are participating in women's enrichment ministry activities.

Special Events
Secures special committees that join together to plan and implement retreats, conferences, banquets, luncheons, seminars, and other special events.

Registration
Works with church support staff to take reservations and sell tickets; is responsible for receiving and handling money for ticket sales at events; provides registration for weekly program activities; provides name tags at all functions.

Missions Emphasis
Works with missions organization (Women on Mission, WMU) to coordinate missions education ministries; provides information and prayer calendars; provides information on special missions prayer emphasis to the church.

Outreach/Evangelism
Is aware of community needs and offers ministry to meet those needs (short- and long-term); encourages seeker-sensitive activities to reach the unchurched.

Prayer
Specifically prays about details and decisions regarding the plans and activities of women's ministry to ensure the stated purpose is accomplished according to God's will; sets up prayer groups as needed; oversees emergency prayer chains.

Art/Design
Helps create appealing flyers, brochures, and news clips for publicity; provides ideas and assistance for platform settings.

Publicity
Handles printing newsletters, and announcements for events and programs (see "Publicity and Promotion," page 116).

Speakers
Oversees selection of speakers for special events; contacts and hosts speakers.

Ministry Network
Oversees the network of ministries (both inreach and outreach) within the church and community in which members may involve themselves in reaching out to others in Christ's name.

New Member Shepherding
Coordinates teams who visit women new to the church to help acquaint them with their new church family, offer assistance as needed, and inform them about areas of interest and service. Team members agree to have at least five touches with each new member assigned to them (visit, phone, mail, invitation to lunch or women's activity, etc.).

Correspondence

Leads a team of women to write personal notes of condolence to bereaved families, notes of welcome to newcomers, and congratulations to women who have just delivered babies in your city, as well as letters of support and encouragement to home and foreign missionaries.

Food

Plans for refreshments, meals, and beverages at events and programs.

Decorations

Works with special events and art/design teams to plan decorations around the theme of the event or study.

Bulletin Boards

Works with women's enrichment ministry director and publicity committee to promote events and programs.

Encouragement/Lay Counseling

Coordinates ministry for women with special needs (crisis, evangelism); provides training for lay counselors.

Secretary

Keeps records; orders materials; serves as historian by keeping scrapbook.

Jesus' Ministry

We have the perfect example to follow as women's enrichment ministry leaders. Jesus was not only a team leader, He was a team member. Jesus ministered with and trained His disciples to carry on His work. He fellowshipped with His team. Jesus prayed with and for them. He did not do everything, but trained others to serve with Him.

Jesus' priority was His relationship with God. Jesus had interruptions as He served, but He met the ministry at hand and accepted it as God's assignment.

Selma Wilson, editor of *Journey*, a monthly devotional magazine for women, shares the following regarding Jesus as leader.

Jesus was not only a team leader, He was also a team member.

Mission Statement

"I have come to do the will of the Father." As leaders, we need to always keep our mission in front of us. Our mission is never about a program, an event, or a resource. It is always about doing the will of the Father. Jesus said the greatest commandment is to love the Lord our God with all our hearts, souls, minds, and bodies (see Deut. 6:5).

Vision

"I have come that [you] might have life and that [you] might have it more abundantly" (John 10:10, KJV). Jesus had a vision for reaching people. We in leadership need a vision for reaching people with the good news of Jesus Christ. That must be central to all we do. Often our vision is limited to having a great event or a great women's program. When this happens, we are not being the leaders God has called us to be. Have a vision for people, not programs.

Focus

Vision and focus are very similar. Vision is about the future. Focus is about what we see right in front of us, that ever-mounting "to do" list. It's all the interruptions we get, all the detours on the journey to our vision. Jesus modeled the journey well. Jesus was frequently interrupted. He had to deal constantly with the religious system. Yet, He never lost His vision. Jesus was a servant leader in everyday life. He took time to minister, listen, heal, and share. Interruptions became opportunities for Jesus to carry out His vision. The interruptions were the will of the Father for His life for that time.

Prayer Life

Jesus modeled the need for prayer and a quiet time with God. If Jesus, the Son of God, needed that time, who are we to think we can live without it? We cannot. We must schedule time each day to be alone, to be quiet before God. This is the key to staying on mission, to keeping our vision, and to staying focused on what's important. In a short amount of time, we can be far away from God's will and mission for us. We must make this a regular part of our lives.

View of Eternity

Jesus had a clear perspective of eternity. He knew His destination. One of the greatest things we can do as leaders is remind ourselves and those around us of eternity. We are truly only passing through this life. This is not our home. If we have an eternal perspective as we live each day, we will be better equipped to stay focused. We are less critical of others, eager to share our faith, better able to give wise advise, and have the energy to do what is before us today. Stop and think on heaven. Read the Scriptures that confirm that we have a home prepared for us. We need to lead with our sites set on eternity.

Commitment

Jesus was committed to do the Father's will all the way to the cross. His last words, "It is finished," have such profound meaning. Jesus had completed the mission the Father had called Him to do. Is that our prayer? God has truly called us to be on mission. We are a part of kingdom business. It is a high and worthy calling. Is it your prayer to have the Father say at the end of your journey in this life: *Well done thou good and faithful servant?*

As a women's enrichment ministry leader, ask yourself, *Who will carry on when I am gone?* Reproducing yourself in others as you follow Christ will ensure that the ministry continues.

[1] Charles Willis, "Volunteer enlistment critical to meet ministry needs," *Indiana Baptist*, August 30, 1994, 6.
[2] Information in this section is adapted from Brad Smith as reported by Ferrell Foster, "Leadership Network nurturing Churches' 'lay mobilization,'" *Baptist Press*, 6 October 1995, n. pag.
[3] William Easum, "Sacred Cows Make Gourmet Burgers," *NEXT* Volume 1, Number 3, July l995, 1-2.
[4] Denise Farrar, "The Mindset of Today's Changing Woman" *Symposium II: Building Bridges Between Christian Women and Their World* (Pasadena: The Women's Ministries Institute®, 1995), 57.
[5] Easum, 2.

Ministry One-on-One

Valerie Howe

Can you name at least one woman who has influenced you spiritually? Women need women in their lives who can identify with their experiences and emotions. Evangelical Christian women's leaders need to know how to implement a mentoring ministry with women in their churches! Why have this sort of ministry? What's involved in beginning and maintaining it? And how will this program be set up in the local church? These questions will be answered in this chapter.

The Bible is our primary resource in implementing mentoring relationships among women in the local church. In keeping the Bible as our guidebook, we will be joining God where He is already working in the lives of women today.[1] Through His Word we can find out what a mentor is, why it's important to have a mentoring ministry in the local church, what type of women God is looking for as mentors, and what's involved in ministering effectively to women. In addition, we can explore the needs of women today and the how-to of meeting these needs through mentoring relationships.

What Is Mentoring?

Let's define the word *mentor.* Bobb Biehl, in his book, *Mentoring: Confidence in Finding a Mentor and Becoming One,* says that a mentor "helps a protégé reach her or his God-given potential. ... Mentoring is more 'how can I help you?' than 'what should I teach you' "[2] That does not mean a mentor does not teach. The Bible specifically says women are to teach other women. This will be discussed a little later, but keep in mind that teaching and modeling are involved in mentoring.

God has a plan for women that will stand the test of time. In some ways it seems that our modern generation has disregarded this teaching on mentoring.

Therefore, many young women, wives, and mothers have never been taught to live godly lives as examples which can be passed on to the next generation. But "down through the centuries, young people have learned most through careful observation of those who are more experienced,"[3] and "throughout human history, mentoring has been the primary means of passing on knowledge and skills in every field and in every culture."[4]

To support this concept of mentoring, Bob and Yvonne Turnbull suggest four keys for mentoring effectively.[5] I have adapted these for our discussion. Combined, they offer a definition of mentoring as well as a guide for us to follow.

There are four keys to mentoring effectively.

Key One: Share Your Successes and Struggles.

When I lost my temper with another church member, I confided my lack of patience to my senior friend, Faye. She had earlier shared with me that she used to have trouble with her temper. When I told her of my situation and that I wondered if I'd ever conquer my temper like she had, she replied, "Honey, just because you're 74 doesn't mean you still don't have to work at not losing your temper. It's just under control." Warning: Don't let sharing your struggles be seen as an excuse for sin. A shared common experience should be a way to move a mentoree toward Scripture for guidance on how to live.

Key Two: Share What You Do and How You Do It.

When I was searching for a way to have a short, meaningful quiet time, a lay renewal speaker came to our church and suggested using *Journey: A Woman's Guide to Intimacy with God.*[6] Mentors can suggest books they have found helpful on child-rearing, marriage, or specific subject matters in which the mentoree needs assistance.

Key Three: Build Skills to Meet Needs.

This is done in obvious and not so obvious ways. For example, my mother-in-law taught me directly how to make a pie crust, but she also taught me indirectly that Kenny, my husband, enjoyed eating her pies. That's why I wanted to learn her method—I had watched him eat her pies.

Key Four: Make Adjustments to Find What Works Best.

Elders have the authority to guide us in making adjustments as we submit to them in humility. They can see some of the pitfalls that lie ahead if we continue on a harmful course. A wise older woman who baby-sat for me once told me I was trying to do too much on my own. "Valerie," she said, "some day you'll learn to receive help." Her evaluation freed me to be able to do just that—receive help!

Each mentoring relationship will take on characteristics of its own, but teaching and modeling will always be involved. Mentoring is ministry one-on-one! It is a great place to start a women's enrichment ministry in the local church. But why is it needed?

Why Have Mentors in the Church?

1. The Bible commands it for women.

Scripture says, "Likewise, teach the older women to be reverent in the way they live, not to be slanderers or addicted to much wine, but to teach what is good. Then they can train the younger women to love their husbands and children, to be self-controlled and pure, to be busy at home, to be kind, and to be subject to their husbands, so that no one will malign the word of God" (Titus 2:3-5). We will look at each phrase of this passage later in this chapter.

2. God calls women to it.

"Those he predestined, he also called" (Rom. 8:30). God knew from the beginning that women would need some instruction on godly living, so He called the older, more spiritually mature women of His church to teach younger Christian women that which is good. This includes single, married, divorced, widowed, professionals, homemakers, and every woman of the church. In her book, *Between Women of God,* Donna Otto says,

> As I look back, I clearly see how God has faithfully provided other older women — messengers, models, mentors — to lead me along, to show me my Lord and Savior, to share the message of His love in flesh-and- blood, hands-on ways, and to help me with the nuts and bolts of everyday living. Woman after woman helped me find Christ and thereby discover rest and hope, peace and encouragement, health and fulfillment in all that God has for me. Each one delivered her message differently, and each one was effective.[7]

3. God qualifies women for the task.

If we "examine the biblical basis for a woman's worth and God's place for her in ministry from the perspective of women as *qualified* for ministry,"[8] we see that women can minister with other women like no one else.

Women are qualified for a number of reasons.
- They have been created in the image of God.
- They are qualified by redemption.
- They are qualified by Old Testament example.
- They are qualified by the example of Jesus.
- They are qualified by the example of the early church.
- They are qualified by Scriptural injunction.
- They are qualified by opportunity.
- They are qualified by the blessing their ministry brings to the entire church.[9]

4. A mentoring ministry will build the church.

Vickie Kraft, author of *Women Mentoring Women,* says,

> "I believe that God's promise to provide gifted persons for the equipping of the church includes His giving gifted women to local congregations. I believe God gives each congregation the gifted women it needs to minister to the unique needs of its women. When older women train

Women can minister with other women like no one else.

the younger women in a vital women's ministries program, not only are the women encouraged, but families and marriages are strengthened and stabilized. … A church without a vital ministry to women is like a home without a mother."[10]

5. There are blessings for the mentor.

One thing that happens in a mentoring ministry is that mentors help other women along in the journey of faith. They also equip younger women with the essentials they need to live a godly life.

In "Packing for the Journey," in *Christian Single* magazine, Deborah Tyler says, "You have to slow down enough to listen; to care. You will have to consider the needs of others and not just your own. But the payoff is significant. As you travel the feminine journey, take time to listen to the beat of another's heart. By doing so your own heart will grow stronger and you'll have more energy for the road ahead."[11]

There are other things that mentoring will do for the mentor. Their own answers become clearer; they will complement and clarify their own understanding; their mentorees will become teachers and mentors; they will refresh and rejuvenate the energy of youth; they will enjoy the satisfaction of a job well done; and they will work on a project with lasting value and eternal significance.[12]

How could Christian women say no to mentoring when God says yes?

Listen carefully. The Bible commands it; women are called to it; they are qualified for it; it builds the church; and it benefits the mentor. How could Christian women possibly say no to mentoring when God says yes?

Oh, how younger women are searching for mature, godly role models — a Sarah, a Naomi, an Elizabeth — to guide them in the truth of God's Word. Women are ordained through Scripture, called of God, and in need of one another. This is why a mentoring program is so vital in women's ministry.

What Is Involved in Mentoring?

Just how do women live out the task of mentoring in daily practical ways? Let's begin with an example. My mother is my mentor. She has given me a godly heritage passed down from her mother and grandmother. She says that her mother lived such a good life and was so kind that she "caught" godly lessons from her. My mother has done the same for me.

My mother has taught me many practical and spiritual lessons. She taught me to pray and to study my Bible daily. These two things alone have led me to know God more fully and to lead others to discover the Jesus I know.

From my mother I learned to love my husband and five children. She taught me to set up a home routine and not to take on too many activities that would spoil my family time.

Mostly, I would say my mother taught me how to live; but mainly, she taught me how to die. For it was she who introduced me to my Lord and Savior. Her favorite verse of Scripture has become one of mine: "I know whom I have believed, and am persuaded that he is able to keep that which I have committed unto him against that day" (2 Tim. 1:12, KJV).

Yes, my mother is my *model*. My mother is my *sister in Christ*, and my mother is my *mentor*, a godly woman just a little ahead of me, cheering me on to victory in Him (see Heb. 12).

According to Lucibel VanAtta in her book, *Women Encouraging Women*, "Mothers and female relatives remain the time-honored and natural choices for role models. But too many miles or transient lifestyles or broken family relationships may separate them from us. … [So] Christian women today are looking for mentors."[13]

What I learned from my mother about mentoring applies to all mentoring relationships. Love your protégé. Be an encourager, affirmer, cheerleader. Be open and honest in sharing with her. Pray for her regularly. Hold her accountable to God's Word. Seek what is best for her. Communicate often. This is what is involved in mentoring.

Who Should Be a Mentor?

To become mentors, women need to pay special attention to the type of woman God calls to this task. "Likewise, teach the older women to be reverent in the way they live, not to be slanderers or addicted to much wine, but to teach what is good" (Titus 2:3).

". . . teach the older women to be reverent in the way they live, . . . to teach what is good" (Titus 2:3).

Reverent in the Way They Live

The word *reverent* comes from the Greek language and describes a priestess serving in the temple of her god in the full-time service of worship. Think of this—women willing to give their whole lives to serving a false god. Christian women who serve the risen Lord should be more willing than these women to count all of their lives as holy, living sacrifices (see Rom. 12:1). This means that cooking and cleaning, resting and exercising, speaking and listening, in addition to studying God's Word and praying are all of consequence in God's kingdom. The reverent life for the godly older women in the local congregation is lived out moment-by-moment and is certainly worth modeling for younger women. These women are easy to spot, for they truly are passionate about their relationship with God and want to share it with others.

Not Slanderers

Older, godly women make younger women feel they can safely communicate their struggles and problems without fear of others knowing their confidences. Christian senior adults communicate appropriate Scriptures instead of inappropriate stories, so that younger women will turn to God's Word instead of speaking in ungodly ways. For example, when mentorees have a problem (or a victory), they can learn to turn from sin (or to praise) and thank God by using God's Word instead of their own words. The more the Word is used, the less chance for gossip. The Greek word for *slanderer* or *malicious gossip* is taken from the root word *diabolus*, which means "devil." Satan uses broken confidences to divide believers. Vickie Kraft says, "A woman who is rooted in a deep relationship with God will not have the overwhelming need to pass on juicy tidbits to enhance her own popularity, and consequently her personal relationships will be protected."[14]

Not Addicted to Much Wine

The Greek term used in this phrase means "drunkard." It could include other addictive behaviors such as abusing drugs, watching soap operas, excessive shopping, reading inappropriate materials, and eating too much. If older women haven't learned how to live life trusting in the Lord rather than these behaviors, they will have little to offer younger women.

Recently through a Christian weight loss program the Lord showed me an addictive behavior I had. Gluttony, to put it bluntly, was my weakness. Through Scripture study and learning to eat only when I'm truly, physically hungry, my focus has shifted from food to God. Now I'm gaining the victory (actually losing pounds) and will someday be free from my slavery to food. Any behavior that takes your mind and focus from God is not in His will. "Escaping reality does not promote biblical living."[15] Older women should avoid escaping reality and teach younger women of faith to avoid this, too.

Teach What Is Good

Like every form of teaching, passing on knowledge must have a goal, some principle or objective that needs to be taught. The goal of mentoring in the case of godly women is for an older role model to teach a younger, willing student how to live a godly life. *Good* in Greek means "morally good, noble, or attractive." The mentor understands what is good and has a working knowledge of Scripture. She knows right from wrong as it is stated in the Bible. In addition, she knows it in principle. A mature woman of faith can guide a younger woman to depend on God's work in her own life to accomplish His purpose. This is the goal of mentoring.

What Should They Teach?

What good things are mentors of God to train or encourage younger women to do to help them depend on God to accomplish His purpose in their lives? "Then they [older women] can train the younger women to love their husbands and children, to be self-controlled and pure, to be busy at home, to be kind, and to be subject to their husbands, so that no one will malign the word of God" (Titus 2:4-5).

Love Their Husbands

If married, mentors can encourage mentorees to love their husbands. The Greek word for love here is *phileo,* the love of human emotion, friendship, and enjoyment. *Phileo* means to truly be friends with their mates. They should have fun, laugh, and enjoy one another. When disagreements occur (and the mentoree needs to know that they will), the mentor can offer suggestions for solving conflicts in marriage. Bob and Yvonne Turnbull have an effective eight-step approach to resolving conflict:

1. Deal with the anger.	5. Define the problem.
2. Set a time to talk.	6. Look for a solution.
3. Establish ground rules.	7. Develop a plan.
4. Pray together.	8. Close the issue.[16]

Love Their Children

If they have children, mentors can encourage mentorees to love their children. In today's society, women need to know that "children are a gift of the Lord" (Ps. 127:3, NASB). Children are not objects to be used or abused. Older women can use their personal experience as well as sensible wisdom to teach younger women "to bring [their children] up in the training and instruction of the Lord" (Eph. 6:4). One practical way to do this is to pray with them for their children and to teach them to pray daily for their families.

Younger women are instructed to teach their children God's Word "when [they] sit at home and when [they] walk along the road, when [they] lie down and when [they] get up" (Deut. 6:7). This takes time. Working moms who are trying to keep their families from drowning financially must be encouraged to find creative ways to do this. They need mentors to stand in the gap between themselves and their children.

Stay-at-home moms seem to have an advantage to teach their children all the time, but weariness and fatigue often set in after days of isolation. A mentor who can pray and counsel, even over the phone, can bring true spiritual healing through Christ to a broken woman.

Be Self-controlled

Jesus said, "I am sending you out like sheep among wolves. Therefore be as shrewd as snakes and as innocent as doves" (Matt. 10:16). Older women need to be alert while being discreetly open in their sharing. They must be willing to be vulnerable to show younger women that they are not alone in their problems and struggles. Mentors are to guide the mentorees to follow the Holy Spirit's leading in everyday situations. This should include using the Bible to encourage the mentorees to give themselves completely to God, as well as to apply to needs as they arise. For example, Nancy, an older friend of mine, told me to praise God when a crisis arose because God inhabits praise, and Satan must flee.

Be Pure

Another thing daughters of faith are to learn is "to be pure." Vickie Kraft speaks well to the issue of purity.

> This characteristic is very significant as it is related to the subject of loving your husband ... [by maintaining] sexual chastity before marriage and fidelity in marriage. ... Every biblical prohibition against sex is of sex outside the marriage relationship. Within marriage it is to be fully enjoyed and celebrated. Indeed, an entire book of the Bible, the Song of Solomon, describes in vivid detail the joys of the marriage relationship. However, marriage was designed as a commitment without alternatives.

> Sex within marriage is an important part of the ongoing relationship between husband and wife. Women need other women to encourage them to understand both the privilege and responsibility of the sexual relationship. A neglect of the physical aspects of marriage can put the relationship at risk. ... Physical relationship is to continue regularly except for a season of prayer for particular reasons (1 Corinthians 7:5). The decision for restraint must be by mutual consent and for a brief

Mentors are to guide the mentorees to follow the Holy Spirit's leading in everyday situations.

time. (And, of course, there are times when for reasons of health there must be abstinence.)

A woman committed to purity and faithfulness in the sexual area honors the Lord and is a blessing to her family.[17]

Be Busy at Home

Managing the home may be a forgotten subject in the church. However, it makes a tremendous difference to a woman's family as well as to God, or He wouldn't have included it in Titus 2:5 as an area for training younger women. Women are to "manage their homes" (1 Tim. 5:14). In the Greek language, this means to be the house despot, total ruler, or to manage the house in such a way that the family is kept in order. In this environment the husband/wife relationship will have a better chance to thrive and grow, and the children will be more at ease.

Basic household skills can be taught by a mentor who has already been there and done that. Skills such as cooking, cleaning, ironing, sewing, planning meals, and managing time wisely are highly useful to young women. For example, scheduling nap time and picking out clothes on Saturday night for church have been invaluable suggestions to me. Laying clothes out the night before a school day also lessens anxiety in the morning. This counsel sounds simple, but what a gift it is to the woman on the go.

Whether married or single, women (and their families) benefit from a well-run home. Just as cups of cold water given in Jesus' name will one day earn a reward (see Matthew 10:42), the mundane tasks of household chores must certainly be of eternal consequence, too.

Be Kind

Being kind involves words that encourage husbands, children, friends, and strangers. It also involves actions that say "I care" to those around.

Mentors find creative ways to express their love. A card, a word of encouragement, a meal, or caring for children are but a few ways to model and instill kindness. They live the command, "Be kind and compassionate to one another, forgiving each other, just as in Christ God forgave you" (Eph. 4:32).

Being kind involves words that encourage.

Be Subject to Their Husbands

If married, mentors can encourage mentorees to submit to their husbands. The Greek word for *obedience* used in the commandment for children (Eph. 5:1) and slaves (Eph. 6:5) is different from the word used for *submit* or *subject* (Eph. 5:22). This is *voluntary submission* — submission given willingly to a husband's leadership. It does not suggest nor state that women are in some way inferior to men, only that they have a different role. It does say that women are to respect their husband's role as head of the house.

This kind of submission is possible only as younger women learn to obey Christ and submit to His authority. Then and only then will they see the benefits that respecting their husbands can bring.

Jesus chose to submit His will to the Father. How much of a higher model or mentor do women need than Christ? When women learn to obey God by submitting themselves to their husbands, the blessing of God will rest on their homes. The home then becomes a place of security, protection, and peace where the women, under their loving husbands' direction, are allowed to grow to their highest potentials.

A wife's submission to her husband includes all the other areas in Titus 2:4-5 that God instructs older women to teach. In loving her husband and children; in being self-controlled, pure, and kind; and in managing the affairs of her home; a woman truly shows she is submissive to both her husband and to the Lord.

Live So the Word of God Will Not Be Dishonored

When older women model and teach the commands given in Titus 2:3-5, "the Word of God may not be dishonored" (NASB). This is true because the younger women who have learned these truths will be beacons to others. The world needs to see such examples passed on from one godly woman to another. Psalm 103:17 says,

> But the lovingkindness of the Lord is from everlasting to everlasting on those who fear Him,
> And His righteousness to children's children
> To those who keep His covenant
> And who remember His precepts to do them.

To a world that is lost and dying, mentors and mentorees alike can honor God's Word and witness to others. Now that's evangelism!

How Do We Get Started in Our Church?

Form a Mentoring Committee

The best place to start is to form a Women's Ministry Mentoring Committee. If the church is not large enough to support a full committee, select two to three dedicated women who are willing to guide the program.

Determine a Time Frame

Select a time to begin that is most convenient for the church. September or October are optimum times. Various schedules will work. Partners can meet once a month for a year. A shorter time frame may fit your situation better. They might meet for six to eight weeks at a time and study the Bible and/or learn some skills which can be taught by one of the mentors or a special guest. Or, the church may want to offer an in-depth study such as *A Woman's Heart: God's Dwelling Place,* or *A Heart Like His: Seeking the Heart of God Through a Study of David,* both by Beth Moore.[18] These studies provide an excellent opportunity for mentoring pairs to study together during the week and then attend the weekly group session.

Donna Otto and Vickie Kraft have developed different plans. Donna suggests a 24-week series in segments from September through May, skipping holidays and school breaks to accommodate moms with kids in school. Vickie recommends a daytime and a nighttime schedule with different course offerings for various interests. It runs in three segments: a fall session from mid-September

When older women model and teach the Bible, younger women will become beacons to others.

to mid-November; a winter session from the week after New Year's to mid-March; and a spring session from late March to mid-May. In the summer it would be nice to plan one or two events where families could be included. The ideas are limitless.

Publicize the Program

Determine the most effective forms of publicity to be used. The mentoring program should be publicized and sign-up opportunities given for at least a month prior to the designated start time of the program.

Possibilities for publicity include newsletters; verbal announcements; church bulletins; brochures; posters; flyers; and newspaper, radio, and television ads.

Compile a Profile Sheet

Prepare a profile sheet for each mentoring participant which will allow older women to be paired with younger women. This profile should include such things as name, address, phone number, personal interests, areas needed in spiritual growth, and what participants want from a mentoring relationship.

Mentoring involves time and effort, but it yields great rewards.

It may be helpful to establish age limits. Vickie Kraft suggests that seniors be over 45, while juniors be under 35. Women between 35 and 45 qualify for either category. Once participants return their completed profiles, the committee can pair women according to their answers. Much prayer must go into this part of the process.

Just Do It

From here on out, just about anything goes. For the pair's first meeting, consider a tea or some other get-acquainted session. A list of "getting-to-know-you" questions may come in handy. Some basics might include: What is your favorite color? food? activity?

Encourage participants to pray for each other regularly and to do things together such as developing a skill, going to lunch, and meeting for Bible study. The important task is to build the relationship. Stay in contact with juniors and seniors to make sure both are fulfilling their commitment.

At the end of whatever time frame you choose (whether 6 months or a year), close with a special time of testimony and celebration for the relationships that have been developed. When you begin the next series, some partners may choose to be paired together again.

If you see that no one else is interested in mentoring in your church, don't be discouraged. Ask God to show you a mentoree or a mentor and get busy. Lucibel VanAtta's book *Women Encouraging Women,* is helpful for this one-on-one ministry.

As women build relationships with one another, a women's enrichment ministry, as well as the entire body of Christ, blossoms and grows. Women are led to the Christ who is their Soon-and-Coming King. Jesus Himself leads them to one another to do the work of building each other up in the faith until He returns. As Christian women, we must heed His command, answer His call, and meet the needs of women inside and outside His church. We must live godly lives so that we can motivate and teach other women to be about His business, too. No matter what age we are, we should always be seeking a mentor as well as others we can mentor.

Mentoring involves time and effort, but it yields great rewards for both older and younger women. It can and should be an incredible adventure!

[1]Adapted from Henry T. Blackaby and Clyde V. King, *Experiencing God: Knowing and Doing the Will of God* (Nashville: LifeWay Press, 1990), 32.

[2]Bobb Biehl, *Mentoring: Confidence in Finding a Mentor and Becoming One* (Nashville: Broadman and Holman, 1996), 19.

[3]Drs. Les III and Leslie Parrott, *The Marriage Manual* (Grand Rapids: Zondervan Publishing House, 1995), 7.

[4]Ibid., 12.

[5]Material in this section adapted from Bob and Yvonne Turnbull, *Marriage Mentors* (Nashville: Lifeway Press, 1995), 19-20.

[6]To order or for more information call 1-800-458-2772.

[7]Donna Otto, *Between Women of God* (Eugene, Ore.: Harvest House Publishers, 1995), 17.

[8]Vickie Kraft, *Women Mentoring Women* (Chicago: Moody Press, 1992), 16.

[9]Ibid., adapted from 16-22.

[10]Ibid., 12.

[11]Deborah Tyler, "Packing for the Journey," *Christian Single,* December 1995, 31.

[12]Parrott and Parrott, 66.

[13]Lucibel VanAtta, *Women Encouraging Women* (Portland: Multnomah Press, 1987), 18.

[14]Kraft, 29.

[15]Ibid., 30.

[16]Turnbull and Turnbull, 68-69.

[17]Kraft, 34. Author, Denise Farrar, *Women's Ministry Symposium IV:* The Women's Ministries Institute®. Used by permission.

[18]For more information about women's enrichment ministry resources contact the Baptist Sunday School Board Customer Service Center at 1-800-458-2772.

Meeting Needs Through Groups

Rhonda H. Kelley

Women need other women! This statement shouldn't surprise any of us. After all, we realize how much we need each other and prove it every day by our actions. For example, women go together to the ladies room. If a woman goes alone to the restroom, she often starts a conversation with a stranger and leaves with "a new best friend." We desire to build new relationships and nurture old friendships.

When the church recognizes that women need other women, the door is opened for exciting new ministries. One way to help women interact with other women is by providing group experiences. Small groups within the church can strengthen the individual woman as well as the corporate body of the church. Through groups, the needs of believers in the church and unbelievers in the community can be met. Let's examine the role of groups in the women's enrichment ministry of the local church.

The Three A's of Groups

Why do most women benefit from group interaction? The support and love of a small circle of friends can nurture a woman in a unique way. Personal relationships help meet several basic needs of most women—acceptance, affirmation, and accountability. These three A's serve as the primary purposes of any women's group within the church.

Acceptance

Women today need a sense of belonging, a confidence that they are a significant part of a whole, an important member of a body. Statistics and trends in divorce, spousal abuse, and sexual harassment in the workplace indicate many women are not finding acceptance. In addition, loneliness becomes a woman's greatest enemy when she senses isolation. Small groups, especially within the church where beliefs and lifestyles are similar, can provide women with acceptance. In words and actions, other women in the group express love, concern, and understanding. Women are strengthened by the acceptance of others.

Elizabeth, mother of John the Baptist, accepted her unmarried cousin, Mary of Nazareth, who later gave birth to Jesus Christ the Messiah. Elizabeth loved Mary despite what other people thought. She praised Mary for her faith in God and befriended Mary while awaiting the birth of her own child (see Luke 1:39-56). Christian women today can offer acceptance and love to others.

Affirmation

A grateful word, a loving hug, or a kind gesture goes a long way with a woman. Encouragement is not just appreciated by women, it is necessary for women to thrive. Members of a group can offer encouragement to one another and promote personal growth. In Scripture, Phoebe was an encourager to Paul (see Rom. 16:1-2) and Priscilla, with her husband Aquila, was an encourager to Apollos (Acts 18:24-26). During the trauma of the crucifixion, a group of women supported Jesus and each other by standing together at the foot of the cross. The affirmation of godly women was crucial to the establishment of the early church. Christian women today are strengthened by the affirmation of others.

Encouragement is not just appreciated by women, it is necessary for women to thrive.

Accountability

A woman may wish to change or desire to reach a goal, and if she senses support from others it may be easier. Whether she is seeking personal or spiritual growth, a woman's self-discipline is developed in part by accountability to others. A Bible study group, a weight control program, or a life support group provides an external checks-and-balances system to supplement internal discipline. Naomi became Ruth's accountability partner in her search for God and a fulfilling life (see Ruth 1:6-22). Women today are strengthened by their accountability to others. Small groups can actually encourage believers to grow closer to each other and closer to God.

Distinct Needs

Almost everyone would agree that life is filled with crises and challenges. While the women of the world face hurt and despair, even the most godly woman has her own needs. These needs are personal and real. They are universal and yet unique to her. They are life-changing and life-ending. The needs of a woman affect every area of her life—physical, social, emotional, and spiritual. The churched and the unchurched have human needs that can be met by God and through the ministry of His church.

In a recent seminar, "The Needs of Women Today," the following were identified as the six most significant needs of women.

1. Salvation and spiritual growth
2. Acceptance and self-worth
3. Family unity
4. Friendships
5. Financial security
6. Crisis care

In his book *His Needs, Her Needs* Willard Harley suggests that the five most common needs of women in marriage are:

1. Affection
2. Conversation
3. Honesty and openness

4. Financial support
5. Family commitment[1]

While you may agree with these conclusions, don't just accept a list of needs developed by another person. If God is leading you to develop a ministry to women, identify the needs of the women in your world and allow God to meet those needs His way. As you perceive common needs, small groups may be a way to effectively meet those needs.

There are several ways to determine the needs of women around you. First, you may be aware of "seen needs." Obvious needs of women may be very clear to you or your leaders. The women in your church may need fellowship, encouragement, and spiritual development. Seek the opinion of a staff member or an outside consultant to help delineate these general needs.

Personal perceptions and expert opinions are helpful, but often you must seek more specific information. "Surveyed needs" add objective data to the personal opinion of "seen needs." It is useful to survey or canvas individuals about their perceptions of what they need most.

The objective of a survey is to gather data from persons other than yourself.

A survey can be formal or informal, general or specific, written or verbal. The objective of a survey is to gather data from persons other than yourself. You may choose to gather information informally from a small number of women by calling them on the telephone or meeting in a focus group. Or you may decide to obtain data formally from a larger number via a written survey or church-wide meeting. (See Survey for Small-group Ministry, page 89.) After you do your survey, be sure to use your results in your leadership team as you plan activities for women, and report your findings to your women and other church leaders.

No matter what method you use to determine the needs of women in your church and community, identify *specific* needs. If you do not clearly define your target, you will never hit it. Always focus your ministry on the needs of the people, not the impact of the program.

In her book *Designing Effective Women's Ministries* Jill Briscoe says, "All I had to do was figure out 'my' needs and how God could meet them and then learn how to press the need button for other women as well."[2] That is the challenge for each of us in developing a ministry for the women of our church. First, we must understand how God is meeting our needs. Then, we must realize how God wants to meet the needs of other women through the activities we offer.

Diverse Groups

There is more than one way to effectively implement a women's enrichment ministry. Therefore, there is not just one list of appropriate groups for women. In order to offer groups that truly meet the needs of the women in your area, answer the following questions.

- Who are the women in your church?
- Who are the women in your community?
- What are their needs?

- What are your available resources?
- What has worked before?
- What has never worked before?
- What are other churches doing to address similar needs?
- What is God leading you to do?

While it is helpful to listen to other people and learn from other churches, be careful to avoid inappropriate imitation. It is essential to the vitality of your work to personalize your ministry. Let your women's enrichment ministry be unique. Establish a one-of-a-kind mentality. Another church is not your church; their needs may not be your needs; their gifts may not be your gifts. Seek wisdom from the Lord to establish groups that will effectively meet the needs of the women in your church and community. Among the most common types of groups are special interest, Bible study, prayer, and support groups.

Be careful to avoid inappropriate imitation of other programs.

Special Interest Groups

Churches today offer a variety of groups specifically for women. Special interest groups often form when a consensus of opinion is shared by several women. These women join together to discuss issues relating to political or social concerns, professional involvement, or personal interests. Some churches have advocacy groups, business organizations, or home management classes. A citizens' awareness group may help inform the women of your church and community about local, state, and national issues as well as suggest appropriate actions they can take.

Bible Study Groups

Bible study groups are key to a growing women's enrichment ministry. Christian women who have a personal commitment to the systematic study of God's Word benefit from group interaction and accountability. Ongoing Bible studies or periodic Bible studies are both effective. Some churches provide more general study while others provide in-depth study. Weekly or monthly, daytime or evening Bible studies can be established. Once the need for a group Bible study has been identified, seek a dedicated teacher, find an ideal time, and determine an appropriate topic for study (see "Tapping Resources for Women's Enrichment Ministry," page 122). Group discussion and teacher interpretation greatly increase a believer's understanding of Scripture.

Prayer Groups

Committed Christian women are women of prayer. While the practice of personal prayer is the privilege of every believer, group prayer is a dynamic way to experience the presence of God. Your women's enrichment ministry should call women to private prayer while offering opportunities for corporate prayer. Prayer groups typically share prayer concerns, form prayer chains, promote prayer events, coordinate prayer partners, and sponsor prayer rooms. The critical need is not to talk about prayer but to pray. Group prayer is a vital tool for personal discipleship and evangelistic outreach. Together our prayers make our cares lighter!

Support Groups

Another effective group provides support. In recent years, support groups have been used in hospitals, schools, community centers, and churches to provide instruction and encouragement. A support group is actually a peer-led group of individuals who share a common need and who meet on a regular basis for interaction. Christian support groups are especially beneficial because members share similar biblical values and uphold Scripture as the definitive guideline for life decisions. In addition, these groups define a clear purpose, meet a specific need, and establish effective leadership.

Christian support groups are beneficial because members share similar biblical values.

Numerous nationwide Christian support groups have developed including Mothers of Preschoolers, Moms in Touch, National Center of Home Education, First Place, and Life Support Groups. Church-based programs may include support groups for women who are divorced, abused, terminally ill, single parents, or unemployed. Support groups can be ongoing or periodic. One church periodically sponsors a "Women in Crisis" series addressing such topics as infertility, job stress, empty nest, mid-life crisis, blended families, death, and grief. These support groups respond to the needs of women in the church but also provide outreach to women in the community. Brenda Hunter noted, "Women always need other women to come alongside and speak their language: the language of the heart and of feelings. We shape each other's attitudes and self-definitions as we converse, and from each other we learn what it means to be female."[3] Look for opportunities to stimulate group interaction among women in your church and community so they can strengthen one another.

How to Begin

Now that you better understand the importance of small groups in a women's ministry, you might be thinking, How do we begin? God may lay a burden on the heart of one woman in your church to start small groups for women. In other cases, the pastor or church staff may develop a vision for the women of the church. There is no "official" way to begin. When God reveals a want to, He will provide the way. The important thing is to start!

If your groups are staff-directed, be sure to include women of the church in the planning. Women's groups by women for women have proven to be most successful. While the church staff is an integral part of the planning, pray that God will raise up women who will volunteer to coordinate the small groups. One woman or a few women may start a women's group. On the other hand, be sure to discuss all plans with your pastor and staff. Coordination with the church calendar will help prevent conflicts and assist in promotion of your groups.

Feel the freedom to structure the groups in your women's enrichment ministry your own way. Keep these suggestions in mind as you start small groups. Use the following checklist as your guide.

☐ 1. Pray for each other and become sensitive to personal needs.

Prayer is key to any ministry, especially during the start-up stage when wisdom and guidance from the Lord are essential. A small prayer group may become the catalyst for other groups.

☐ 2. Survey the women of your church.

In order to identify felt-needs and design appropriate groups, listen to the women of your church and community. In doing so, you may choose not to duplicate other groups and start new ones. In any case, your local needs should determine your agenda, not someone else's model.

☐ 3. Develop Bible study groups as a foundation.

A personal commitment to the Lord and His Word should be expressed through participation in systematic Bible study. Christian women are interested in spiritual growth and enrichment which can be promoted through group involvement. Bible study is the most common type of women's group.

☐ 4. Keep missions and community outreach a priority.

Women's enrichment ministry should include missions groups with a focus on exciting and relevant education, awareness, and involvement.

☐ 5. Work closely with your church staff.

Responsibility for leadership of the church has been assigned to staff members. Seek their wise counsel. Women's groups are part of the total church program.

☐ 6. Find and train dedicated leaders.

God will raise up women to give leadership to the groups in your church. Be alert for willing workers and assist them in training for their job. Be particularly sensitive to women who have not held a leadership position before. New ministries often uncover new leaders.

☐ 7. Hold a church-wide special event to promote the groups.

Many women will respond to a one-time activity before making a longer-term commitment. A special event attracts a larger number of women who can learn about small-group opportunities. Perhaps a "Preview Day" would be appropriate to overview options offered during this time frame. Offer information and register women on this day.

☐ 8. Develop nurturing relationships.

Small groups, especially in a large church, encourage personal contact and close friendships. While your women's enrichment ministry will respond to the needs of the whole body, small groups can focus one-to-one on each individual.

☐ 9. Work in harmony with other church groups or programs.

Your church may have ongoing groups in place. Try to complement the mission of other groups while clearly defining your group's purpose. A diversity of groups shouldn't compete but should strengthen each other.

☐ 10. Stay positive, focused, and pray, pray, pray!

Any Christian work can become overwhelming and discouraging. Keep your attitude positive and your vision clear. And, above all else, pray without ceasing for yourself, your small groups, and your church.

Abundant Blessings

When shared with a group, joys are multiplied and sorrows are divided. The blessings of group interaction among women are many. Don't let the women of your church and community miss the blessing of personal relationships!

Personal Blessings

Personal blessings are abundant to those involved in women's groups. A woman will experience limited growth personally and spiritually without interaction with other believers. When supported by members of a group, a Christian woman will flourish and be fruitful. Group meetings become a highlight of life, not just another appointment on the calendar.

Ministry Blessings

Churches with dynamic women's enrichment ministries that provide small groups are most often growing churches. If the women's groups are successful, then all other women's events will be strengthened. Specific blessings such as genuine enthusiasm, numerical growth, diverse participation, and prospective members will be the natural result of well-planned women's groups. The blessings to individual women and the total women's ministry are unlimited.

Conclusion

As you develop women's enrichment ministry in your church, resist the temptation to start a group for every woman's need. Instead, seek God's guidance, pray for wisdom, be sensitive to needs, recognize helpful resources, and start simply. You don't have to do everything at once. The success of your women's groups will become an investment in the spiritual growth of women in your church and community. The needs of women in your area can effectively be met in large part through the development of appropriate small groups. God bless your efforts to reach women for His glory!

[1] Willard Harley, *His Needs, Her Needs* (Tarry Town, N.Y.: Fleming H. Revell, 1986).
[2] Jill Briscoe, et al., *Designing Effective Women's Ministries* (Grand Rapids: Zondervan, 1995), 17.
[3] Brenda Hunter, *In the Company of Women* (Sisters, Ore.: Multnomah Books, 1994), 23.

Survey for Small-group Ministry

As a Christian woman, what is your greatest personal need or the area in which you would like to experience growth through being involved in a small group?

_____

_____

What are the three most prevalent needs of your closest non-Christian friends that we can address in a small-group ministry?

1. _____

2. _____

3. _____

Thinking about the women of our church, what concerns do you share for them and what do you feel are needs that can be addressed in small-groups?

_____

_____

List three pressing needs or issues our community is facing. How can the women of our church help address these problems through small-groups?

1. _____

2. _____

3. _____

What is your dream for the women of our church?

_____

_____

_____

_____

Small-group Ministry Plan Sheet

This plan sheet is designed to assist you in beginning small groups within your women's enrichment ministry. Once you conduct and compile the results of your survey, use this form to move forward in your planning.

Determine Priorities
Decide what needs expressed by the women in your church are priorities you will be able to meet through your small-group ministry.

1._____

2._____

3._____

4._____

5._____

Set Goals
What will you focus on this year based on the priorities listed above?

1._____

2._____

3._____

Determine Actions
What small groups will you offer that will help you reach your goals?

Small Group	Date	Person Responsible
_____	_____	_____
_____	_____	_____
_____	_____	_____
_____	_____	_____

Future Plans
Looking ahead, what would you like to include in next year's plans?

1._____

2._____

3._____

Special Events: Programs or People?

Jaye Martin

Why did you have your last women's special event? Was it because you have always had it? Was it because you heard that First Church had a similar event and it was successful there? Did you find a great logo and plan something to go with it?

Every special event should be planned to meet needs of women. Often, it is easier to copy an event we have heard about than it is to determine the needs of our women and program to meet those needs. Lots of programs and flashy brochures can be impressive, but are lives being changed?

Needs of Women

Let's begin our discussion of special events by looking at some of the needs of today's women.

Balance

Anytime you can help a woman with one or more of her responsibilities, she will juggle her busy schedule to be there. For instance, give her tips on how to manage her time wisely, simplify her life, establish a quiet time, study the Bible and apply it to her crazy schedule, be a better wife or a great mom, or be a Proverbs 31 woman in the world today. Help her find some answers to bring balance to her life.

Stress Relief

No matter what season of life a woman is in, she is often stressed. I used to think it was just in large cities. However, after talking to women from all walks of life in small towns and large cities, I have discovered that most women are under stress. Oh, there may be a different degree of stress, but it is still there! Offer women an opportunity to get away from the daily grind and they will come. Give women some ways to handle stress and they will be there. Help them discover a new perspective on life, and they will be grateful.

Purpose

Far too many women don't know their purpose in life. Help them find a purpose! God has a plan for each woman and it is our job as women's enrichment leaders to help them know God, grow in their walk with Him, and share their walk with others. Women need to understand that they are uniquely gifted for service; and that until they are bearing fruit, they will not find meaning in their lives. Help women discover their spiritual gifts as well as their talents. Then give them places to use those gifts and talents to further the kingdom of God. When you do, you will find you have women who are fulfilled, joyful, and ready to serve.

Relationships

Significant relationships can be difficult to come by in today's society. Before television and portable stereos, folks used to sit around and chat. What a novel thought. And when women would talk, things had a way of working themselves out. Aunt Polly would give her perspective, Granny would tell how it was in her day, and before the evening was over, wisdom had been shared and relationships had been strengthened. Women need each other. Women like to share and need to know there are women out there who care about them and the things going on in their lives. Provide ways for your women to get to know each other and time to sit and chat. They will build mentoring relationships that will change their lives forever.

Once you determine that you are going to meet the needs of women, pray and ask God to show you which needs to address and when.

Planning special events is something Jesus addressed in Scripture.

Scriptural Basis for Planning Special Events

Planning special events is something Jesus addressed in Scripture. In Luke 14:16-23, Jesus tells of someone planning a great banquet. In this passage, Luke gives us two basic principles about planning. Verse 16 says, "Jesus replied: 'A certain man was preparing a great banquet and invited many guests.' "

Preparing

Preparation is crucial to the success of any event. Anyone who has ever planned a banquet knows how much work goes into it! Much planning has to take place before the banquet or event happens. In planning events for our women, we want to ask God for direction on what to plan and when. When God gives us direction, we must follow through on what He tells us to do. So, preparation is a key to planning special events.

Inviting

The other truth we see in Luke 14:16 is the importance of inviting. Why prepare a banquet if we are not going to invite anyone? But notice what Jesus tells this man about whom to invite. First, we can assume a group has already been invited because Jesus tells us the man "sent his servant to tell those who had been invited, 'Come, for everything is now ready' " (v. 17). This group makes a lot of excuses why they cannot come. One had bought a field and had to go and look at it. Another had just bought five yoke of oxen and was on his way to try them out. Still another had recently married and couldn't come. The servant came back and reported this to his master. The master then ordered his servant to go out quickly into the streets and the alleys and invite everyone he could find. After the servant did this, there was still room. The master then told him to go further down the roads and the country lanes and invite others to come in so that the house would be full.

Notice how much more information Jesus gives us on inviting than on preparing. We usually spend more time on preparation than we spend on who is coming to our events. That may be because we usually expect to have the same crowd each time. After all, these events are for those actively involved in women's enrichment ministry, and maybe one or two others from the church will come. Yet, Jesus shows us the importance of reaching out to those who might not be included. In fact, it seems Jesus sent some personal invitations to these folks.

Although it is perfectly in order to mail brochures and make phone calls, it is most important that we send women out to personally invite inactive women to come. It may be a personal invitation to the woman who works at the school, or the neighbor two doors down, or the lady who does your hair. Jesus goes on to tell us there will be lots of silly excuses but not to let it stop us. He tells us to keep on inviting until we get others to come. Maybe the clerk at the grocery store would like to be included. And the new mother down the street may need a friend. Then there is the lady whose husband just died who would probably be glad to get out of the house. These and many others need our touch.

We live in a nontouch world. A world where women have too many responsibilities, are under too much stress, have no purpose, and have few relationships. All these women and many more are just waiting for someone to care, waiting for someone to stop and notice they exist. Through events, we can reach out to women and show them a new world where Christ can provide them a new perspective, allow them to meet new friends, and give them meaning to life.

Purpose of Events

A special event is different from an ongoing small group. A special event is a one-time event that focuses on a particular issue or theme. Usually we do extra things to make it special but the purpose of providing special events is still to reach women for Christ. Specifically, the purpose of an events ministry is to:

- reach women for Christ;
- mature women in the faith;
- involve women in service through spiritual gifts and talents;
- support and undergird the church.

Having a purpose gives direction and makes planning easier. In order to reach women, there must be something significant that they want to experience at the event. Then, not only do we reach them, but we disciple them so that they grow closer to Christ and His ways. As women come to Christ and grow in their relationships with Him, they will want to serve. Planning special events through women's enrichment ministry will help them learn to use their gifts

We usually spend more time on preparation than we spend on who is coming to our events.

and talents for the Lord. This supports the church as well as the women. After all, Christ commands us to "go and make disciples."

R-E-A-C-H Women

What this means is that special events might need to be thought of a little differently. To R-E-A-C-H women, here is what needs to happen:

R-ethink everything!

E-ncourage nonchurched women to attend.

A-nnounce! Announce! Announce!

C-hallenge members.

H-oly Spirit led—pray and expect God to move!

R-ethink Everything!

We begin by rethinking everything we do! First we need to think like the women who are without Christ. What motivates them? Why would they want to come to one of our special events? We have already looked at a few things we know are important in women's lives and these become ways to bring them to a meaningful relationship with Christ. Helping women prioritize their lives; helping them handle stress; giving women a sense of purpose; and helping them build lasting, meaningful relationships with family members and other women are just a few of the things women are looking for.

Perceived Needs vs. Real Needs

What do women in the world today think they need? Some of these perceived needs include more money, material possessions, a husband (or a new one if they are married), children (or new ones if they have children), fun, and fellowship. Basically, women want a quick fix for their stressed, lonely, and hurting lives. They want help for today.

Let's think about what they really need. We know the answer; we know they need Jesus. Jesus is the master at meeting needs. He gives help for today and hope for tomorrow. However, since women don't understand they need Christ, how do we reach them? We begin by rethinking some things.

Titles

We have to be careful when we name our events. Titles like "Only Jesus," "Missions Alive," and "He Lifted Me" won't be attractive to many women, especially non-Christian or unchurched women. We must rethink our titles. Instead of "A Study of 1 Corinthians 13," why not "True Love," or "A Love That Never Ends," or even "The Love of Your Life"? Make your themes and titles something your non-Christian neighbor would want to come to.

Greeters

Every time you have a special event, greeters or hostesses need to be smiling faces at the door that make women feel welcomed. Be careful not to embarrass guests by putting them on display or by giving them a name tag when no one else is wearing one. Let them know you care. For example, pair them up with someone they can sit with who will introduce them to others.

Groups

We all know how difficult it is to walk into a group where everyone knows everyone and we know no one. Sometimes new groups need to be started so that women will feel good about being involved. As you plan a special event, make sure everyone will feel comfortable walking into the event or group.

Rethink some things. Do some new things. The "15th Annual Event" tends to leave the impression that this may be the same group that's been together year after year. Use this as a subtitle following a fresh, new major title.

Invitations

There are many good ways to ask women to respond to Christ without having to walk to the front of the banquet hall or assembly room. Make it comfortable to respond. We want to have the opportunity to explain the difference that Jesus can make in their lives. Unchurched women may not be familiar with our traditional "come to the front" invitations.

Response cards (see sample on page 101) provide a wealth of information for follow up. Ask the women to let you know what they thought about your event and include things such as:
- I would like to be on the mailing list for your women's events.
- I would like to know more about what this church can do for me.
- I have some spiritual questions. Please have someone call me.
- I would like to talk to someone about knowing Christ personally.
- Today, for the first time, I asked Jesus to be my Lord and Savior.
- Today, I recommitted my life to Christ.
- Today, I committed to a special ministry of _____ for Christ.

Once women respond, it is easy to follow up after the event. Another good idea is to have them bring the card to a prayer room or give it to a hostess. This way they can be counseled before they leave.

E-ncourage Nonchurched Women to Attend

We have already looked at some of the needs of women in the world, but there are a few other things we can do to encourage nonchurched women to come to our special events.

Price Breaks

Most women love a good deal. After you figure your cost per person for your event, let your members pay a little more and your guests pay a little less. For instance, if the event will cost $25 per person, why not let the members pay $30 each and guests pay $20 each?

No Late Fees

If there is to be a late registration fee, do not require your guests to pay it. Many guests will sign up at the last minute. We want them to attend, not resent having to pay a penalty for registering late.

Go to "Away" Locations

As nice as it is to use church facilities, it is also good to go places away from the church. These can be retreat or conference centers, office buildings, or even public parks. They don't have to cost a lot of money. This provides a neutral, nonthreatening setting for visitors.

Giveaways and Door Prizes

Publicize that there will be giveaways and door prizes. What is it about those tote bags that everyone loves? If tote bags are too expensive to give away, they can be sold and a few given as door prizes. One of the best things about registering for door prizes is that it provides a name, address, phone number, and the name of the friend they came with. Use the back of the event ticket for the information. These are drawn for door prizes and used for easy follow-up to the event.

Special Emphasis

Other ways to encourage nonchurched women to come are to have special days such as friend days, neighbor days, teacher appreciation days, family days, work-associate days, brown-bag lunch or picnic days. These special events may attract someone who hasn't been before. Recognize those who are new and give them extra privileges such as sitting close to the front, or getting their food first. Whatever works!

A-nnounce! Announce! Announce!

Publicity

After we have completed our rethinking process and thought of ways to encourage nonchurched women to attend, we are ready to publicize our special event.

There are numerous ways to let women know you are having a special event. See "Publicity and Promotion," (page 116) for ideas. But don't stop with these. Let this list serve as a starting place and be creative!

No matter what types of announcements you choose to make, the best form of publicity is person-to-person. Most people come by personal invitation. Church statistics tell us that 95 percent of the people who attend a church for the first time do so because someone invited them. This will also hold true for your women's enrichment events. So, whatever kind of advertising you choose, it only supplements the person-to-person invitations that you and your members make to those you come in contact with. "Inviter evangelism" is easy to do for most everyone. We saw this in the passage in Luke about the Great Banquet. Jesus wants us to invite everyone to come so that His house will be full! So, how do we do this? Read on ...

C-hallenge Members

Challenge members to get out of their comfort zones and invite unchurched women to attend the event. As always, people need to be challenged to reach out to others. Most of us tend to stay in our comfort zones. Providing incentives can help members do what they already know they need to be doing.

Bring a Friend

Have a "bring a friend" event. You can even go so far as to have an event where no one can come unless they bring a friend (someone not from your church). Believe it or not, this provides great incentive and gets everyone active.

Reserve Seats for Members with Guests

Create a reserved section at the front for those members who bring a friend and for other guests who come alone. Let everyone know in advance that those who go the extra mile will be rewarded with great seats.

Have a Reception

Have a special reception for members with visitors just prior to the event. Have church staff members and women's leaders there to greet and to mingle. You might even provide members with guests a different nametag or something else to identify them during the main event. The reception is also helpful to let guests know your church is there to minister to them.

Make Special Introductions

As long as you are careful not to embarrass anyone, you can do some meaningful recognitions during the event. Just having them stand (members and guests) is good.

Take Photographs

Have a time for photographs to be taken with special friends. This is great because the member can tell the guest in advance they want to have photos made together. This especially works well with family members.

Provide Evangelism Training

Provide training for your women in lifestyle witnessing, friendship evangelism, and building relationships. (See resource section at the back of this book for materials.) Help your women learn to give their testimonies and share their faith. When the event comes, they will be ready to respond.

H-oly Spirit Led ... Pray! and Expect God to Move!

Are you expecting God to move at your special event? If you are not, then you probably will not notice when He does. We demonstrate our anticipation of God's movement by doing some things in advance.

Train Leaders to Pray

Throughout the planning process, prayer needs to be a major part in all you do. Do not assume your leaders know how to pray for an event. Teach them how to pray and what to pray for. Teach them to look for God's movement and direction.

- *Pray Individually* You must be the role model. Pray for God to move. Pray for every person who will help you plan. Pray for your attitude and the attitudes of others. Pray for your members to bring their friends. Pray that these friends will come to know God in a personal way. Pray continually.

- *Pray Together*   Not only is it important to pray alone, it is important to pray together as a group of leaders. Share what God has already begun to do. Share needs and struggles of those in the group. Pray together before you plan anything. God will bless.

Train Leaders to Disciple/Mentor Other Women

As you plan your special event, the mentoring process is going on. When women observe how other leaders respond or react to details, the spirit in which changes are made, and the flexibility of leaders, they learn to be Christlike. Provide times together for your women. Do not have a lot of women doing planning by themselves.

Train Leaders to Witness

We have already looked at the importance of teaching women to share Christ with others. Your events will take on new meaning when your leaders experience the joy of sharing their faith with others.

Listen to God

Expecting God to move, praying privately, and praying together are all important, but so is listening to God. If you do not listen, you will miss what He is trying to tell you. It may be about the location of an event or the speaker; it may even be about the name tags. Listen to what God tells you. Prayer is two-way communication. Spend some time listening to God, and then act on what He tells you to do. And you, my friend, will be led by the Holy Spirit.

Moving Toward the Event

Let's consider other details that move us closer to the event.

Determine the Need

Who are you planning this event for? What are the needs of the group? How much will the group be able to afford? Will your budget be able to underwrite the expenses? What is the best day of the week? What time of the day? What is the purpose of your event? What is the best location?

These are all questions that need to be answered before speakers are booked or dates set. A special event for a group of young single mothers will look different from an event for young single adults. Make sure you are realistic about how much women can afford to pay. If you book an expensive speaker and an expensive hotel, your costs will increase greatly. No matter how great your event is, many will not be able to come unless scholarships are provided.

Figure the Budget

Estimating the budget is really easier than you might think. Here are a few things you need to know to begin.

1. How much will the facility charge? If you find yourself at your church, you have just saved money (in most cases). If you use another facility, ask for an estimate on all charges that might come up. Things such as easels, overhead projectors, microphones, and skirted tables can run the bill up quickly.

2. How much will the food (meals, snacks, water stations) cost? Be sure to include the gratuity charges. Most hotels charge a set percentage for their staff, and this changes the cost significantly. Be sure to remember that your speakers (and maybe others) will not be paying, so their expenses need to be absorbed in participant fees.

3. How much will your brochures or fliers cost? Will you be mailing anything? What other printing charges will there be (prayer cards, evaluation cards, programs, notepads, bookmarks, handouts, tickets, maps)? Printing charges vary depending on the type of paper, number of colors of ink, amount of material printed, whether it goes to the printer copy-ready, and more. If all your printing can be done at the same time, it usually saves you money. A printer can help you estimate the costs.

4. How much will you be able to spend on decorations? You will probably need some type of centerpiece for the tables, a backdrop for the stage, and various decorations on registration tables and in other areas.

5. What will be the fees or honorariums of the speaker(s) and worship leader(s)? What other expenses will there be for these people (travel, accommodations, meals, miscellaneous expenses)?

6. How many women are you expecting? The more you have, the less it will cost each person because more will share in the cost of the event. How much are your women expecting to pay? You may be able to start by estimating what you feel each will be able to pay, then see where you are on your budget. To estimate the budget, add all your expenses. Divide by the number of "paying customers" you anticipate, and see where you are. This gives you the price each person will have to pay. You may come up with an amount double what you think the group will be able to afford. It is already time to cut back, and you have hardly begun! Here are a few places to consider cutting back.

- *Location or extras* Bring your own sound crew and equipment (easels, overhead projectors, etc.). If this doesn't help, find a cheaper location. Keep asking others for ideas.
- *Menu* See what the facility managers can do for you. Cut snacks down to water stations, or ask to bring in canned sodas or homemade cookies.
- *Printing* Print the brochures in one color on colored paper; cut the mailing and depend on your women to get the word out, cut all those last-minute handouts or limit the number of pages; cut the printed program—either do without it or scale down. You will be surprised how much you can save in printing.
- *Decorations* Use something someone has already paid for. Plan to sell what you use to regain the costs. You may even be able to make a few dollars on these. The more time you spend reaching women, the less you will be concerned about the decorations.
- *Speaker fees* The truth of the matter is that women are more likely to come to an event because they are involved in the planning than to hear a big-name speaker. This is not to say God won't use her, but be sure it is God calling you to invite that particular speaker.

How are you doing? Are you closer to where you need to be financially? Total your new expenses and divide by the number of women you think will pay.

Developing a realistic budget is important in planning a special event.

Take this amount and add 10 to 20 percent for your per person rate. Also, figure what would happen if you did not have as many sign up as you thought. Will the percentage you added cover it? Will there be any church budget money used to get the price down? Keep figuring until you have a workable budget. Keep your leadership and the church staff informed about your expected expenses and income. If you bring them along with you, they will be more likely to be there for you if you need help later. (See Sample Conference/Retreat Budget, page 112.)

Enlist the Speakers

Before you think about enlisting a speaker, be sure you (not someone else) have heard her. Listen to tapes, ask for references, and call them to get a feel for who they are. Ask for strengths and weaknesses. Speakers are best found by networking with other women's enrichment ministries. Call around and find out who others have had in their churches that they were pleased with.

When enlisting a speaker, there are some basic things that need to be covered. Use this as a checklist. It is also a good idea to put it in writing. You will not be the only event she will be praying about.

- ☐ Purpose—communicate this clearly to the speaker
- ☐ Topic—what you want her to speak about
- ☐ Schedule—number of times she will speak, how long she will speak each time, exactly where in the program she will speak, and whom she will be following
- ☐ Location—church, retreat center, other; include the place where she will be spending the night (if applicable). Most speakers prefer to room alone to have time to prepare for their presentation.
- ☐ Participants—who will attend, their ages, their needs, and the number of women you expect
- ☐ Payment—fees or honorarium; let her know which of her expenses you will cover. Prepare the check before the event and present it to her at the event closing.
- ☐ Prayer — ask her how you can best pray for her
- ☐ Photo and biography — if you are planning to use her biography and photograph, let her know when you will need it; also, return it to her at the event or shortly thereafter
- ☐ Person — make sure she has the name of the person (you or someone else) she can contact if she has any needs or questions

At the Event

You are finally here! Relax! Keep smiling! Be flexible and calm. Have a great time and keep praying!

God has been with you, and He will continue to be. Don't let the program or event get in the way of the people you are ministering to. If you have been thorough and have followed the Holy Spirit's leading, chances are you will have a special event that will help women with their priorities, pull them away from their hectic schedules, give them a purpose, and help them develop significant relationships. And you, my friend, will have been a success. Give God the glory!

After the Event

Begin immediately to plan for your next event. Compile information from the Response Card and Event Evaluation you ask women to complete at the event (samples provided on the following pages). Follow-up on decisions made at the event. Use the other information to begin praying over your next special event. Ask God to direct you and the other leaders in your church so you can continue to meet women's needs through your events.

Response Card

☐ I would like to be on the mailing list for your women's events.
☐ I would like to know more about what this church can do for me.
☐ I have some spiritual questions. Please have someone call me.
☐ I would like to talk to someone about knowing Christ personally.
☐ Today, for the first time, I asked Jesus to be my Lord and Savior.
☐ Today, I recommitted my life to Christ.
☐ Today, I committed to a special ministry of _____ for Christ.

Comments about this event: _____

_____

_____

Prayer Request: _____

Name: _____

Address: _____

City/State/Zip: _____

Phone Number: _____

Event Plan Sheet

This plan sheet is designed to assist you in planning a special event for your women's enrichment ministry.

Notes	*Date to be completed*	*Person responsible*

☐ Purpose

_____ _____ _____
_____
_____
_____

☐ Title/Theme

_____ _____ _____
_____
_____
_____

☐ Budget

_____ _____ _____
_____
_____
_____

☐ Location

_____ _____ _____
_____
_____
_____

☐ Speaker(s)/Musician(s)

_____ _____ _____
_____
_____
_____

☐ Promotion

_____   _____   _____
_____
_____
_____

☐ Menu

_____   _____   _____
_____
_____
_____

☐ Decorations

_____   _____   _____
_____
_____
_____

☐ Printing

_____   _____   _____
_____
_____
_____

☐ Honorariums/Expenses of guests

_____   _____   _____
_____
_____
_____

☐ Evaluation

_____   _____   _____
_____
_____
_____

Event Evaluation

1. How did you hear about the event?
   ☐ Brochure   ☐ Radio   ☐ Friend   ☐ Newsletter
   ☐ Conference Leader ☐ Newspaper   ☐ Other: _____

2. What is your overall evaluation of the event?
   ☐ What I expected   ☐ Better than I expected   ☐ Less than I expected

3. What was your favorite/most helpful part of the event?

   _____

   _____

4. What was your least favorite/helpful part of the event?

   _____

   _____

5. How can we provide a better event?

   _____

   _____

6. What topics would be most beneficial for the next event?

   _____

   _____

7. Other comments:

   _____

   _____

8. Optional:
   Name:_____

   Address: _____

   City/State/ZIP: _____

   Phone: _____

Conferences and Retreats

Merci Dixon

Planning your first women's conference or retreat is similar to planning for your first child. You anticipate wondrous things, yet you are apprehensive. You are filled with excitement, yet you are uneasy. You look forward to a great day, but with mixed emotions. And when the day arrives, you are filled with all the hope of the psalmist when he declared to God, "My hope is in you" (Ps. 39:7).

For the past 10 years we have conducted two very special annual events in our church just for women. One of the events is a spring women's conference, and the other is a fall women's retreat. We define these two events separately, even though many church leaders use the terms interchangeably.

Women's conference — a one-, two-, or three-day meeting held at the church for the purpose of ministering to women; listening to godly speakers; growing in relationship to Christ; and worshiping through Christian music, eating, and sharing together.

Women's retreat — an overnight, weekend event held in a retreat center or encampment for the purpose of spiritual growth and bonding together. The weekend includes skits, music, speakers, small-group prayer times, sleeping (or not sleeping!), and eating together.

The purpose of this chapter is to help you develop effective conferences and retreats. We will give you a blueprint to keep you on target. No two conferences or retreats will be the same, but with each event there are essentials that cannot be overlooked. These necessary ingredients include: prayer, planning, publicity, priority, and purpose. We will look at each of these individually.

Even though much of this material is directed toward the women's enrichment ministry coordinator, it also applies to committees and leaders.

Prayer

Please don't attempt anything for the Lord without first seeking His direction. Before you contact the first speaker or contract for a retreat center, you need to pray for God's guidance. Jesus said it best: "Ask and it will be given to you; seek, and you will find; knock and the door will be opened to you" (Matt. 7:7). God has something special just for your women. Even when you get ideas from other places, don't rely on them to make your conference successful—rely on God to do what He wants to do in your midst.

Planning

Rely on God to do what He wants to do in your ministry.

The following time line will help you plan your conference or retreat. Personalize it for your event, but do not shortcut your planning.

One to Two Years Before the Conference or Retreat

☐ Set the tentative date for the conference or retreat. Be sure you have the event set for a time when there are no conflicts on your church calendar. It would be wise to check school and community calendars and sporting events. This is especially important in retreat planning. Since a retreat takes women away overnight, the fewer the conflicts, the better the attendance.

☐ Determine your budget. This includes expenses and income. What will the event cost? How much will the church underwrite? How much will the participants have to pay? (See Sample Conference/Retreat Budget on page 112.)

☐ Contact the first keynote speaker. If the date works for her, contact other speakers. Do not contact all of the speakers at the same time (to avoid conflict). Using two or three keynote speakers has worked better for us because different personalities minister to differing needs. Adjust the date if speakers are not available to be with you on your first choice of dates. Ask them if they require an honorarium. Even if the speaker does not have a set amount, be as generous as your budget will allow.

☐ In the case of planning a retreat, lock in on a location and reserve it. Some popular facilities fill up fast.

Four to Six Months Before the Conference or Retreat

☐ Decide on a theme, based on Scripture. From the theme, develop message titles, seminar topics (optional), decoration themes, and publicity plans.

☐ After you have decided on 12 to 15 seminar (small group) topics, pray about who God wants you to ask to lead. After you have seminar leaders in mind, give the list to your pastor, other staff member, or fellow committee member to pray about. Once you have both prayed and are assured that the leaders are right for your event, contact each one on the same day. Contacting all of your seminar leaders on the same day discourages suggestions about who could lead. Too much input can be confusing.

☐ Write your keynote speakers and let them know how plans are progressing. Give them all the information you can. Ask what you can do for them as they prepare to come.

☐ Decide about offering scholarships and the process for advertising and obtaining scholarships.

Two to Three Months Before the Conference or Retreat

☐ Send out registration brochures.

☐ Begin working with your committees. The following committee structure has been helpful to us in planning our conferences and retreats. Retreat committees will not be as structured or detailed as conference committees. A retreat should be much more relaxed and will not require as many planning groups. Even so, to ensure a good response from your women, get as many as possible involved in planning.

• Program chairwoman—the women's enrichment ministry director/coordinator; coordinates the event and is in charge of the program, speakers, music, and all other chairwomen; sets up meetings with committees as needed; monitors spending in order to maintain budget guidelines.

• Decorations committee—responsible for putting up and removing all decorations (or selling them after the event). This includes decorating for the meals, all displays set up during the conference or retreat, decorating the bathrooms, and any other extra decorations in any part of the facility to add a special "woman's touch." This is most important to women, who tend to look at details. It will convey you are glad they came!

• Prayer committee—responsible for contacting women who would be willing to pray daily for the needs of the speakers, the committee chairwomen, the weather, those attending, and the facilities before and during the event. There is nothing too trivial to pray over! This committee might also want to prepare a prayer guide.

• Food committee—responsible for planning an attractive menu. You may need one or two meals, depending on the length of your conference. For sure, meals are a critical element on a retreat. This committee is also responsible for refreshment centers set up with light snacks such as coffee, cokes, and mints.

• Lodging committee—responsible for making arrangements for lodging. For a conference, this might just be for out-of-town leaders. For a retreat, this committee's responsibilities include setting up lodging for leaders and participants.

• Secretary/registration committee—responsible for participant registrations; childcare registration (if offered); correspondence to registrants; all monies received; and keeping up with requests for lodging. You may wish to budget money to pay this person if you do not have a support staff in your church.

• Childcare committee—as registrants request childcare (optional), this committee will make the necessary preparations. Childcare registration should be closed two weeks before the event to allow for adequate preparation.

• Publicity committee—responsible for all publicity except registration brochures. Publicity can be through local newspapers, the state denominational paper, on Christian radio stations, or on television. See "Publicity and Promotion," page 116, for ideas.

• Booklet committee— responsible for preparation of the program booklet. This booklet contains the schedule, speaker's outlines, Scripture references, information about the speakers, and places to take notes.

• Packet committee—responsible for the free packet given to each guest (pen, program booklet, tissues, breath mints, key chains, etc.). Check with local businesses for giveaways and door prizes. Include a list of donors in the packet. This

To ensure a good response, get as many women as possible involved in planning.

committee will need to order packets at least three to four months before the event.

- Transportation committee—plans transportation as needed for speakers and participants.
- Book store committee—sets up and runs the book store; receives suggestions from speakers about resources to make available through the store. Ask speaker (if she brings and sells her own books) or book store provider for a percentage of sales (10 percent is a good standard) if you sell their books.
- Counseling committee—prepares or obtains decision cards, tracts, church information, and other follow-up materials. Trains women to counsel.
- Audiovisual committee—obtains audiovisual equipment as needed.
- Greeters—responsible for greeting women and directing them to registration, book store, childcare, and seminar rooms.
- Follow-up committee—calls or sends letters to those who attended from outside the church. Contacts those who made decisions at the event.

☐ Request facilities (rooms), food, publicity and printing, audiovisual equipment, and childcare as needed (see form on page 113).

Two Months Before the Conference or Retreat

☐ Contact speakers and seminar leaders and give them a deadline to have their outlines for the program booklet. Also give them encouragement and direction about the philosophy of the conference and what is expected of them.

☐ Make all motel and airline reservations for guest leaders.

☐ Work individually with each chairwoman about her responsibilities. Even though group meetings may seem better, you can save time by working individually. This also facilitates the decision-making process.

☐ Finalize the schedule and confirm that all details are being handled.

One Month Before the Conference or Retreat

☐ Contact musicians: soloists, instrumentalists, music leaders. Give them a copy of the program and verify their responsibilities.

☐ Make plans for a pre-event reception/prayer time. This reception or prayer time is normally held the afternoon or evening before the conference or retreat and includes speakers, chairwomen, workers, and musicians. The reception can be in one of your women's homes or at the church. This is a special time of dedication and prayer for the event.

☐ Send an invitation to all seminar leaders, keynote speakers, committee chairwomen, workers, and musicians asking them to come to the reception.

☐ Make plans for a meal after the conference or retreat. The purpose of this meal is to feed out-of-town guests before they leave and to have something special for your workers before they clean up the facilities.

☐ Send a second mail out (optional) to advertise the conference or retreat and make an appeal to send in registration forms.

☐ If you don't have all the speaker's and leader's outlines, call and request them. The booklet needs to be printed and reproduced so they can be assembled at least two weeks before the conference or retreat. If you do your own printing, be sure to order plenty of supplies to complete the booklet, including paper, binders, and cover pages.

☐ Plan three or four workdays for your women during the last two weeks before the conference or retreat. Put these dates on your church calendar. Clear the dates with your booklet, packet, and decoration committees, because these are the ones who will need the most help. Publish a sign-up sheet for the workdays and circulate it around the church.

Two Weeks Before the Conference or Retreat

☐ Finalize plans with your committee chairwomen, making sure details are covered and they have plenty of volunteer help.

☐ Confirm reservations for speakers and leaders.

☐ Contact women in your church to act as hostesses and to introduce the speakers.

☐ Complete the program booklet and assemble.

☐ Stuff the packets and store them until the event.

☐ Write guest speakers and leaders, telling them how many women are registered for the event and their individual seminars, and sending them a copy of the program booklet.

☐ Complete program plans.

☐ Consider not scheduling any extra women's programs the week prior to the event.

☐ Give the financial secretary or church treasurer an itemized list of honorariums, including speakers, singers, musicians, sound personnel, and conference secretary.

The Day of the Conference or Beginning of the Retreat

Try to relax and enjoy the day! It's in God's hands and He gets all of the credit and the glory!

After the Conference or Retreat

☐ Send thank you notes to all who helped with the event including door prize and gift bag donors and church staff (secretary, maintenance, hostess, etc.).

Publicity

While prayer and planning are two of the most essential ingredients to a successful conference or retreat, you cannot overlook publicity. You must get the word out!

One of the most effective ways to publicize is through personal invitation. After you have developed your theme and enlisted your speakers, you will want to produce an appealing brochure you can send to as many women as possible.

Your target audience might include:
- Women in the church
- Women on mailing lists from outside the church (from previous conferences, meetings, or retreats, or from another churches' mailing list)

• Women in churches in your state (obtain this information from your state denominational offices)

Another way to publicize the event is to send correspondence to all the churches in your area asking them to publicize the event. You will need to follow up the correspondence with a phone call, making sure someone has agreed to help you. If a church has an active women's enrichment ministry, they may be less likely to participate because of their own activities. Nevertheless, encourage their support.

As was previously mentioned, you can advertise in your local newspapers, your state denominational paper, on Christian radio, and on television. All of these advertisements need to include the essentials: what, where, when, why they should come, and how they can get more information.

Maintain an appropriate focus on your conference or retreat.

Develop an active file for free advertising: community calendars, listener-supported radio stations, public service announcements. Utilize women in your church who are experienced in public relations. If no one is, don't let that stop you from contacting media outlets in your community.

Don't wait too late to advertise! A month before the conference is not sufficient time!

Don't advertise too early! Four months before the conference gives them plenty of time to put the brochure aside and forget (unless you are going to follow up later).

See "Publicity and Promotion," page 116, for more information on publicity.

Priority

Maintaining an appropriate focus on your conference or retreat is important. It is easy to get sidetracked. Here are a few suggestions that will help you keep your priorities in order.

Focus on God's Goodness.

Count your blessings and consider the women who are going to benefit from the event! Talk about it often; pray about it always; keep the goal in front of your leaders at all times. Plan a day for prayer and fasting.

Support Committees

Support the committee chairwomen and let them do their jobs. If it's not exactly the way you would do it, that's OK.

Keep Your Head!

When you have 20 to 30 women working on a project, disagreements and cross purposes occur. Everyone looks to see how upset the leader is going to get. Remember that you set the tone.

Set Goals

Set a number goal of women to attend, stick to that goal, and close registration when you reach it. This is an unpopular thing to do, and no one likes that responsibility, but you do a disservice to the ones who have registered early when you crowd in more than you had planned for.

Be a Servant

As a church sponsoring a conference or retreat, your role is that of a servant (or servants). When Simon criticized the woman for weeping and washing Jesus' feet with her tears, Jesus told him, " 'I came into your house. You did not give me any water for my feet. ... You did not give me a kiss. ... You did not put oil on my head' " (Luke 7:44-46). When the women attend your event, take the posture of a servant, not of Simon the Pharisee.

Purpose

Why is it so important to mention purpose? Isn't the purpose to have a conference or retreat? Isn't the purpose to get through the event with no major catastrophes? Isn't the purpose to stay within the budget?

There can be a lot of purposes, all good, but the most important purpose for having a conference or retreat for women is to bring honor and glory to the Lord!

What brings honor and glory to the Lord?
• Changed lives and restored homes.
• A time of spiritual restoration for women.
• Seed planting resulting in salvation.
• God receiving all the credit.

How can you go wrong planning and conducting a conference or retreat with that as your purpose?

When women attend your event, take the posture of a servant.

Sample Conference/Retreat Budget

Conference/Retreat Expenses

Arrangements

Facilities	$250.00	
Food (includes food for workers during planning)	2550.00	
	Total	$2800.00

Hospitality

Hospitality (Reception)	$350.00	
Packets (printed bags, tissues, lotion, novelty items)	1200.00	
Cookbooks	800.00	
Photo expense (photographing conference/scrapbook)	100.00	
Plastic name tag covers	200.00	
Miscellaneous expense	150.00	
	Total	$2800.00

Program

Honorarium (instrumentalists, soloists)	$800.00	
Honorarium (keynote speaker, seminar leaders)	3000.00	
Transportation and lodging for guest leaders	1900.00	
	Total	$5700.00

Public Relations

Newspaper advertisement	$400.00	
Radio advertisement	400.00	
Statewide mail out (postage)	500.00	
Printed materials (brochures and program)	800.00	
Postage (newsletters, registration information)	200.00	
Miscellaneous publicity	200.00	
	Total	$2500.00

Decorations

General decorations	$ 1200.00	
Sanctuary decorations	250.00	
Displays and bulletin boards	150.00	
Miscellaneous decorating expense	150.00	
	Total	$1750.00

Childcare

	$1000.00	
	Total	$1000.00

Miscellaneous

Receptionist during event	$ 150.00	
Maintenance/moving during event	300.00	
	Total	$ 450.00
	TOTAL EXPENSES	$17,000.00

Conference/Retreat Income

750 Ladies @ $20.00	$15,000.00
50 Ladies @ no expense (speakers, music, scholarships, no shows)	
Women's Ministry Budget	$ 2,000.00
TOTAL INCOME	$17,000.00

Women's Ministry Request Form

Date Requested: _____

Event: _____   Date of Event: _____

Leader: _____   Leader Phone: _____

Calendar Request
- ☐ date _____
- ☐ time _____
- ☐ room(s) _____
- ☐ number attending _____

Work Request
- ☐ set-up _____
- ☐ piano _____
- ☐ other _____

Media
- ☐ taping needed _____
- ☐ sound system _____
- ☐ other _____

Audiovisual
- ☐ overhead _____
- ☐ film projector _____
- ☐ VCR _____
- ☐ other _____

Records
- ☐ addressed envelopes _____
- ☐ labels _____
- ☐ mailing list _____
- ☐ other _____

Printing
- ☐ how many? _____
- ☐ type of paper _____
- ☐ color(s) of ink _____
- ☐ date needed _____
- ☐ information sheet and sample(s) attached _____

Food
- ☐ paper goods _____
- ☐ drinks _____
- ☐ food _____
- ☐ time(s) needed _____

Bulletin
- ☐ date to appear _____
- ☐ information attached _____

Newsletter
- ☐ date to appear _____
- ☐ information attached _____

Monthly Calendar
- ☐ month to appear _____
- ☐ information attached _____

Supplies (how many?)
- ☐ Bibles _____
- ☐ childcare cards _____
- ☐ note card _____
- ☐ postcards _____
- ☐ event evaluations _____
- ☐ stationary _____
- ☐ visitor cards _____
- ☐ decision cards _____

Conference/Retreat Plan Sheet

Determine Purpose:
Decide what needs expressed by the women in your church and community are priorities you will be able to meet through this conference/retreat. State the purpose in two to three sentences.

_____

_____

_____

Timetable
One to Two Years Ahead   Person Responsible
☐ Set date   _____
☐ Determine budget   _____
☐ Contact keynote speakers and musicians _____
☐ Reserve location   _____

Four to Six Months Ahead
☐ Decide on a theme based on Scripture   _____
  (to support the purpose you stated above)
☐ Choose seminar topics and leaders   _____
☐ Write keynote speakers   _____
☐ Decide if and how to handle scholarships _____

Two to Three Months Ahead
☐ Mail registration brochures   _____
☐ Begin meeting with committees   _____
☐ Request facilities, rooms, food, audiovisual _____
   equipment, childcare, publicity,
   and printing needs

Two Months Ahead
☐ Contact speakers and request outlines   _____
☐ Make lodging and transportation   _____
   arrangements for speakers
☐ Continue working with committee   _____
   chairwomen
☐ Finalize schedule   _____

One Month Ahead
☐ Contact musicians and speakers and provide _____
   copy of program
☐ Plan pre-event reception and prayer time _____

□ Send reception invitation to seminar
   leaders, speakers, musicians,
   committee chairwomen, and workers   _____

□ Plan post-conference/retreat meal
   for workers   _____

□ Send second mailing of brochure   _____

Two Weeks Ahead

□ Finalize all details for volunteer workers   _____

□ Confirm reservations for speakers, leaders,   _____
   and musicians

□ Complete and assemble program booklet   _____

□ Prepare registration packets   _____

□ Write guest speakers and leaders;   _____
   include program booklet

□ Complete program plans   _____

□ Request checks for honorariums   _____

Day of Conference/Retreat

□ RELAX and enjoy the day!

After Conference/Retreat

□ Send thank you notes to all who helped,   _____
   including door prize and gift bag donors
   and church staff

□ Compile evaluations and begin planning   _____
   the next event

Publicity and Promotion

Gerry Sisk

Whenever and wherever someone or something imparts hope, joy, peace, and passion, the news will travel. It is as true today as it was two thousand years ago that there will be excitement when Jesus is in the house. When a ministry changes lives and homes, it changes churches. When a women's enrichment ministry offers a program built on the Titus 2 mandate for women, God's Word will be honored.

The greatest challenges facing women's enrichment ministry are (1) creating an interest in the ministry, (2) communicating the opportunity to be a part of the ministry, and (3) conveying a heartbeat of the ministry while competing for time within the busy pace of life for most women.

Certainly, the term marketing creates an ambivalent response within the church family. However, it cannot be disputed that God has left the church the responsibility to go and tell others the great things the Lord has done. To be a good steward of that message, it is necessary to utilize every available tool to convey the opportunity to be a part of a Bible-based, life-changing women's enrichment ministry. This chapter serves as a beginning point in developing an effective publicity and promotion plan.

Questionnaires

If a women's enrichment ministry is just beginning, an option for publicity and a way to get women to accept ownership of the ministry is through a questionnaire mailed to every adult woman in the church. Most people love to be asked for a personal opinion. In addition, a letter from the leadership of the women's enrichment ministry, or, in some cases, from the pastor, explaining the heartbeat of the ministry, its goals, and its Scriptural basis and purpose, can be invaluable.

The design of the questionnaire should be adapted to the personality and needs of the local church body. Such issues as ideal times, frequency, and themes for a ministry can be addressed through the questionnaire, as well as asking for comments and questions. A self-addressed, stamped envelope or panel on the flier will guarantee the largest response. If budget does not allow postage-paid return mail, ask women to return the questionnaires to a designated location at the church. After the questionnaires are returned, compile the information and assimilate the ideas into your women's enrichment ministry. (See Survey/Questionnaire, page 46.)

Mail Outs

To effectively use the mail to promote women's enrichment ministry, develop a computer database. If a computer is not available, a written record of church members, visitors, and prospects provides a basis for mail outs. In addition, a list of people who have requested information on special events should be included for mail outs which publicize events and programs.

Let's look at several options. Information in all mail outs should be complete and consistent.

Mail outs can be effective in promoting women's enrichment ministry.

Fliers

Different programs and events can be publicized by utilizing various types of mailings. A flier is usually printed on only one side and in one color. It is most effective when presented on colored paper, selected for its appropriateness for women, the event, the purpose of the event, and other details such as season of the year. Check fliers for accuracy regarding details, spelling, and grammar. When printing fliers, it is usually cost effective to print enough to mail and distribute within the church. Place them in strategic locations and distribute them through church groups. Design fliers that are attractive enough to reproduce on card stock to be placed on doors and walls (place in grippers, if available). Obtain permission from appropriate leadership prior to distributing the fliers in organizations in the church. Minimize cost by printing fliers as a self-mailer with the return address of the church and an address panel on the back if you are requesting a response. This will eliminate the need for a return envelope.

Postcards

To minimize cost even more, limited amounts of information can be conveyed by postcard. Cards 5½" by 4¼" are effective. They are large enough to be noticed but small enough to place on the refrigerator or desk as a reminder.

Brochures

For annual conferences or special seminars, a trifold brochure is effective. A conference normally requires more information than can be conveyed in a flier. Seminar topics, dates, speakers, length and description of workshops, registration deadlines, child care, and food information should be included. A well-done brochure does not have to be expensive; use colored paper to draw attention if you are limited to black ink. Multiple ink colors and attractive clip art can enhance the message if it does not clutter the presentation. Most important, however, are the accuracy and clarity of the text. The reader depends upon the credibility of the information published. Accuracy and careful, thorough planning go hand in hand.

Include your brochures in church guest/new member packets or with packets used in outreach efforts.

Church Newsletters

If a church produces a biweekly or monthly newsletter, announcements regarding the women's enrichment ministry should be routinely submitted. The format, details, location within the publication, and style of the announcements should be varied to avoid visual repetition. Information should be kept brief and to the point, while always answering the basic who, what, when, where, why, and how questions. Occasionally include a personal testimony of how God used the ministry to change a life. Always obtain permission before publishing a personal testimony. When printing capabilities allow, a personal photograph adds to the impact of the testimony.

Women's Enrichment Ministry Newsletters

Other modes of promotion within the church and within the ministry itself include weekly, monthly, or quarterly women's enrichment ministry newsletters. Newsletters can be mailed to women who are members of the church, as well as those who may have visited the church or participate in a women's enrichment ministry event. Newsletters can include details on special events, opportunities to serve, and encouragement to take part in the ministry.

Area-wide Mail Outs

When addressing universal needs, an occasional area-wide mail out may be effective. Lists of residents can be purchased from direct mail services. When purchasing a list of names and addresses, it is possible to set the criteria, such as age of addressees, number/age of children, number of female adults in the home, mile radius from church, etc. These mass mail outs can be expensive but well worth the investment when the ministry event target's a specific need.

Posters

Posters serve as eye-catching ways to publicize events. Use colorful, sturdy materials so the posters will be noticeable and durable. Posters and brochures can be placed in area grocery stores, pharmacies, retail stores, and other businesses—with permission, of course. Be sure to remove them when the event is over.

Book Markers and Business Cards

Bible or book markers made of card stock may be inserted in the order of service on Sunday. They may include a verse around which an event is planned or the verse upon which the women's enrichment ministry is built. Inclusion of clip art and attractive paper and ink colors make the book marker a constant reminder of what God is doing.

Small business cards with information about the women's enrichment ministry are easy for members to carry and hand to those they meet during the week. Include dates for major events and a phone number to call for more information.

Ministry Calendar

Another useful tool for women's enrichment ministry is a ministry calendar. Often, the calendar can be incorporated into a monthly or quarterly newsletter or flier. It is useful when the calendar is kept small enough to be displayed on a refrigerator or desk. Keep the calendar's text readable.

Weekly Bulletin

Within the church family, utilize the order of worship or weekly bulletin. Information should be submitted in a timely manner, honoring print deadlines and media format. Attractive and appealing clip art is helpful in catching visual attention. Anticipate and answer questions the reader or listener might have. When publicizing only basic information, list a telephone number or voice mail information line to address additional questions. If the information published is regarding a weekly event, the format and presentation of the event should be changed often. Otherwise, the reader becomes so accustomed to the visual that effectiveness is minimized. Variety in presentation lends itself to impact.

Other Church Publications

In addition to the weekly bulletin, explore all other publications distributed within the church. Some churches publish a weekly Sunday School information sheet, a midweek communication handout, or special event list. Women's enrichment ministry information should be included, with permission, in every available publication. Use of every outlet lends itself to effective communication at a minimum cost to the ministry and the church. As previously mentioned, publication deadlines and formats differ from church to church. Be aware of those and work closely with the people producing print material.

Word-of-Mouth

The potential for written tools for publication and promotion may vary with the size, location, and personality of the local church. However, the most effective tool is present in every church—word-of-mouth! The leadership of any women's enrichment ministry must be able to convey clearly accurate dates, times, and purposes of meetings through announcements within the ministry. Share the next three months of events at every Bible study or special event. Issues such as child care, cost, and dress should be resolved prior to communicating the event. Overcommunication of basic information is impossible. It is neither necessary nor desirable to deal with details orally; however, the who, what, when, where, why, and how should always be clearly defined prior to announcing or publishing information. Women should be encouraged to invite other women within the church, neighborhood, work environment, or family.

The most effective tool for publicity is word-of-mouth.

Invitations can be designed and handed out when women share information about the ministry with others. Generic invitation cards can be printed and used for various events if they are designed so the specific information can be filled in by hand.

Phone blitzes can be fun for members and also help get the word out to lots of people within a short amount of time. Some church offices have several lines so many calls can be made at the same time.

Announcements

Announcements through Bible study classes and from the pulpit are helpful. In order to use those avenues, however, it is imperative to operate through the correct channels of authority. When asking others to make announcements, provide the information in writing, so there are no misunderstood or incorrect details. Keep copies of all information shared. Oral communication is insufficient if not reinforced.

Testimonies

The first responsibility regarding publicity and promotion of a women's enrichment ministry is to help the women in the church know how the ministry impacts lives for Jesus Christ. With this awareness, the next responsibility involves reaching the community for Christ. Each community is unique in its composition and personality. However, every community has the need for Jesus Christ. There are many avenues available to personally share God's Good News with the community.

Personal testimonies are equally as effective as leadership announcements. Prior to an annual event such as a conference, seminar, mission study, or Bible study session, testimonies of lay women whose lives have been changed by prior conferences or sessions are very effective. These lay leaders can share in Sunday School classes, Bible study groups, or other areas of ministry within the church. As women hear how others have found peace and power for daily living, the visibility and the viability of the ministry increase.

If your church uses video screens, have a video made featuring some of the women involved in women's enrichment ministry. Show this before, during, or after the morning and evening services.

There are many avenues available to personally share God's Good News with the community.

Church Marquee

The church marquee is an effective tool for promotion. Whenever women's enrichment ministry begins a new session, holds a special event, or wishes to offer an invitation to a function, the church marquee is a 24-hour bulletin board. The message should be brief, mentioning dates, times, special guests, and a telephone number. The message should be changed often to avoid becoming ineffective. If a telephone number is listed for information, that number should be answered by someone who can give additional details regarding the event. The phone system should, if possible, include a recording stating the office hours for the telephone number, should the person calling not reach a staff member, employee, or volunteer.

Community Bulletin Boards and Public Service Announcements

In addition to the marquee for local notification, many communities have area newspapers, radio, and television stations which offer free community bulletin board information and press releases. Contact each outlet for the name of the person in charge of public service announcements. Deadlines for receipt of the material to be promoted varies with individual outlets; requirements range from 15 to 30 days prior to the event. Most outlets require press releases and announcements be generated on official church letterhead, listing the name and phone number of a contact person in case additional information is necessary.

Public service announcements are just that—a service; there is no guarantee they will be printed or announced. However, most local outlets are exceptionally gracious in working with churches to get information into the community.

When composing a public service announcement, brevity is important. The material should be written to be clearly understood by those who are unchurched as well as by those who attend church regularly. Dates, times, purpose, cost, child care, and meal information are important details. If the guest speaker or vocalist has local or national recognition, his or her name should be included. Any other information needed can be obtained from the contact person.

Public service announcements are an untapped resource in reaching the community with program information.

Advertising

In addition to public service announcements, radio stations, newspapers, magazines, and television/cable stations offer paid advertising packages. Some offer lower prices for increased advertising in any combination of ministries. Most communication outlets have specialists who will take the basic information and create the graphic layout for the ministry. Proofs are available prior to printing and/or broadcasting. Those proofs should be viewed and carefully examined for accuracy of content and visual design. When running advertisements in the newspaper or on the radio, factors such as publication date as related to event date, high listener times on the radio (i.e., driving to and from work), and frequency of the advertisement should be taken into consideration. Remember that the community is most interested in events and programs which address universal needs such as parenting, marriage, and personal, practical issues.

Denominational Associations

Another wonderful outlet for sharing news of women's enrichment ministry events and programs is through the publications of denominational associations. Local associations are eager to share the news of the church and its ministry to disciple women. Deadlines and format for submittal may vary from association to association and should be requested well in advance of the event to be publicized.

When a women's enrichment ministry begins with the purpose of fulfilling the Titus 2 mandate of women teaching and counseling women, lives are changed, hearts are encouraged, and homes are strengthened. Though women are busy with jobs, homes, and other responsibilities, a vibrant ministry which offers lifestyle application of God's Word is exciting news! Women want to know and will make sure others know that God's Word and God's people make a difference in a demanding, sometimes overwhelming, society. As cold water is to a thirsty soul, so is good news. And, good news travels fast!

Tapping Resources for Women's Enrichment Ministry

Having an understanding of the resources available for your women's enrichment ministry will be invaluable as you begin and develop your ministry with women. This brief chapter is devoted to making you aware of the types of resources that will serve you well. Resources include print material, video and audio resources, and maybe the most valuable of all—human resources. The lists provided are by no means complete. You are encouraged to build on the material in this chapter and develop a personal resource list that will serve you and your women's ministry. Your resource list will grow as your ministry grows.

Contact the Discipleship and Family Adult Department by mail: LifeWay Christian Resources, MSN 151; 127 Ninth Avenue, North; Nashville, TN 37234; by telephone (615) 251-2278; or by FAX (615) 251-5058 for information about resources and ministry development for single adults, senior adults, families, men, and women. Also for information regarding discipleship, First Place, criminal justice ministry, and life support resources.

1. Resources

The resources in this section are available from the Customer Service Center, MSN 113; 127 Ninth Avenue, North; Nashville, TN 37234. Fax orders to (615) 251-5933; email customerservice@lifeway.com; order online at www.lifeway.com; or call toll-free at 1-800-458-2772 from 7:30 a.m. to 5:30 p.m. (Central Time), Monday through Friday. Listings include a product number for easy reference when ordering.

Journey (monthly devotional magazine)

Breaking Free: Making Liberty in Christ a Reality in Life,
> Beth Moore (11 sessions)
> Workbook #0767391128
> Leader Kit #0767391756
> Audiocassettes #076739111X

Living Beyond Yourself: Exploring the Fruit of the Spirit,
> Beth Moore (10 sessions) #0767392752

A Woman's Heart: God's Dwelling Place, Beth Moore (11 sessions)
> Workbook #0805498362
> Leader Kit #0805498265
> Audiocassettes #0805497978

A Heart Like His: Seeking the Heart of God Through a Study of David,
> Beth Moore (11 sessions)
> Workbook #0767325966
> Leader Kit #0767326539
> Audiocassettes #0767326520

The Financially Confident Woman, Mary Hunt (4 or 8 sessions)
> Workbook #0767390725
> Module #0767336003

In My Father's House: Women Relating to God As Father,
> Mary Kassian (6 sessions) #0767335732

Life Lessons from Women in the Bible, Rhonda Kelley (6 sessions)
> #0767335740

The Vision of His Glory: Finding Hope Through the Revelation of Jesus Christ,
> Anne Graham Lotz
> Workbook #0767391160
> Leader Guide #0767391179
> Leader Kit #0767391764

Heaven... Your Real Home, Joni Eareckson Tada (8 sessions)
> Workbook #0805497749
> Leader Kit #0805497528

Shelter from the Storm: Hope for Survivors of Sexual Abuse, Cynthia Kubetin
> and James Mallory (12 sessions)
> Workbook #0805499792
> Facilitator's Guide #0805499806

New Faces in the Frame, Dick Dunn (2, six-session studies) #0805498176

MasterLife, Avery Willis and Kay Moore (4 books, six sessions each)
> *MasterLife 1: The Disciple's Cross* #0767325796
> *MasterLife 2: The Disciple's Personality* #076732580X
> *MasterLife 3: The Disciple's Victory* #0767325818
> *MasterLife 4: The Disciple's Mission* #0767325826

First Place: A Christ-Centered Health Program
> Member Notebook #0767326091
> Leader Guide #0767326105
> *Nine Commitments* Videos #0767394070

Bible Study Packs:
    Living the Legacy #0767335724
    Pathway to Success #0767331737
    Giving Christ First Place #0805499954
    Life that Wins #0805499938
    Life Under Control #080549992X
    Pressing On to the Prize #0805497757
    Everyday Victory for Everyday People #0805499946

Leadership

Jesus on Leadership: Developing Servant Leaders, C. Gene Wilkes (6 sessions)
    Workbook #0805493506
    Leader Kit #0805493514
    Leader Guide #0767329481
Serving God: Discovering and Using Your Spiritual Gifts, Ken Hemphill
    Video Kit #0767322509
    Workbook #0767322517

Prayer

Whispers of Hope, Beth Moore #0767392787
Watchman Prayer Ministry, Larry Thompson
    Planning Kit #0805499601
    Prayer Guide #0805499628
In God's Presence, T.W. Hunt and Claude V. King (Everyday Discipleship, 6 sessions) #0805499008
Disciple's Prayer Life, T.W. Hunt and Catherine Walker (13 sessions) #0767334949

Counseling

WiseCounsel: Skills for Lay Counseling, John W. Drakeford and Claude V. King (13 sessions)
    Workbook #0767326156
    Leader Guide #0767326768
DecisionTime: Commitment Counseling, Leonard Sanderson and Arthur H. Criscoe (6 sessions) #0767391799

Witnessing

Learning to Share My Faith, Chuck Kelley (6 sessions) #0805498648
Witnessing Through Your Relationships, Jack R. Smith and Jennifer Kennedy Dean (12 sessions)
    Workbook #0805498931
    Leader Guide #0805498923
Meeting Needs, Sharing Christ: Ministry Evangelism in Today's New Testament Church, Don Atkinson and Charles Roesel
    Book #0805498427
    Workbook #0805498400
    Leader Guide #0805498419

2. Events

Information is available on a recorded message by calling (615) 251-2277. Or, you may write to the Discipleship and Family Adult Department, MSN 151; 127 Ninth Avenue, North; Nashville, TN 37234.

Single Adult Labor Day Getaways
Crossroads (Single Adults 45+)
Senior Adult Chautauquas
Festivals of Marriage
Toward a Growing Marriage Seminars
Living Proof Seminars (Beth Moore)

3. Baptist State Conventions

Many Baptist state conventions have a person assigned to women's ministry. Call your state convention office and record this person's name, address, and telephone number for later use. Make sure your name is included on the state mailing list so you can receive information on training and enrichment events.

4. Missions Organizations

North American Mission Board
4200 North Point Parkway
Alpharetta, Georgia 30202-4174
(707) 410-6000

International Mission Board
Box 6767
Richmond, Virginia 23230
(804) 358-0504

Woman's Missionary Union
P. O. Box 830010
Birmingham, Alabama 35283-0010
(205) 991-8100

5. Other Organizations

MOPS International, Inc.
(Mothers of Preschoolers)
1311 South Clarkson St.
Denver, Colorado 80210
(303) 733-5353
FAX (303) 733-5770

Leadership Network
2501 Cedar Springs LB-5
Dallas, Texas 75201
(800) 765-5323
FAX (214) 969-9392
(Leadership Network has a monthly FAX (*NET FAX)* and periodical (*NEXT)* containing ministry information from various leaders and denominations.)

Moms in Touch International
(Organization of mothers who intercede for their children and pray that schools may be guided by biblical values and high moral standards.)
P.O. Box 1120
Poway, CA 72074-1120
(619) 486-4065

Christian Schools and Home
 Schooling
127 Ninth Ave., North, MSN 182
Nashville, TN 37234-0182
(615) 251-5749

Samples of Organizational Models

Women's Enrichment Ministry as Umbrella

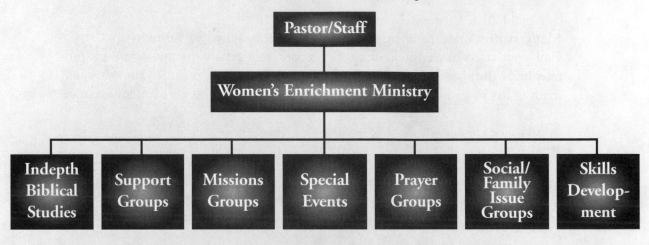

Pastor/Staff

Women's Enrichment Ministry

- Indepth Biblical Studies
- Support Groups
- Missions Groups
- Special Events
- Prayer Groups
- Social/ Family Issue Groups
- Skills Development

Women On Mission and Women's Ministry Blended

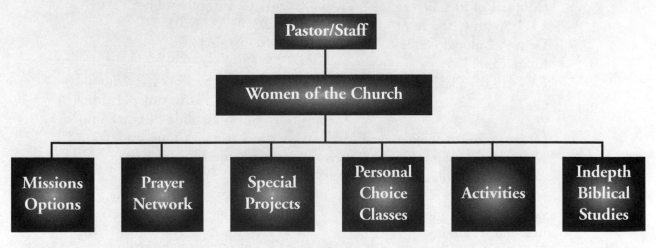

Pastor/Staff

Women of the Church

- Missions Options
- Prayer Network
- Special Projects
- Personal Choice Classes
- Activities
- Indepth Biblical Studies

Women On Mission and Women's Ministry Side by Side

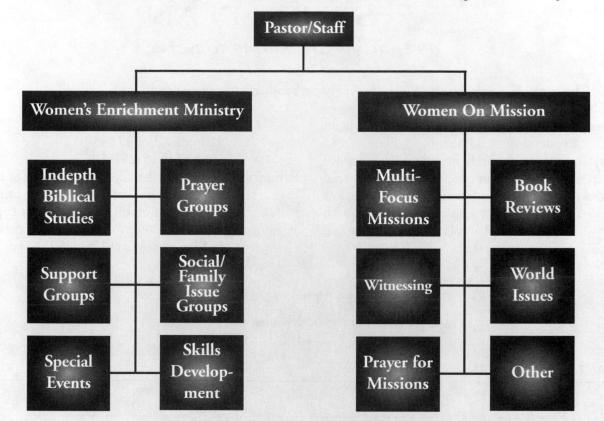

Pastor/Staff

Women's Enrichment Ministry

- Indepth Biblical Studies
- Prayer Groups
- Support Groups
- Social/ Family Issue Groups
- Special Events
- Skills Develop- ment

Women On Mission

- Multi- Focus Missions
- Book Reviews
- Witnessing
- World Issues
- Prayer for Missions
- Other

Women On Mission as Umbrella

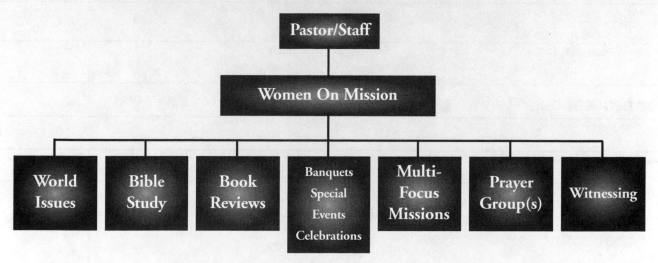

Pastor/Staff

Women On Mission

- World Issues
- Bible Study
- Book Reviews
- Banquets Special Events Celebrations
- Multi- Focus Missions
- Prayer Group(s)
- Witnessing

CHRISTIAN GROWTH STUDY PLAN

Preparing Christians to Serve

In the **Christian Growth Study Plan (formerly Church Study Course)**, this book *Women Reaching Women* is a resource for course credit in **Adult** Leadership Diploma Plan and Understanding the Church Emphasis and Service Ministries Diploma Plan. To receive credit, read the book, complete the learning activities, show your work to your pastor, a staff member or church leader, then complete the following information. This page may be duplicated.

Send the completed page to:
Christian Growth Study Plan
127 Ninth Avenue, North, MSN 117
Nashville, TN 37234-0117
FAX: (615)251-5067
For information about the Christian Growth Study Plan, refer to the current Christian Growth Study Plan Catalog. Your church office may have a copy. If not, request a free copy from the Christian Growth Study Plan office (615/251-2525).

WOMEN REACHING WOMEN
❏ Women's Enrichment Ministry (LS-0034)
❏ Church Leadership (LS-0083)

PARTICIPANT INFORMATION

Social Security Number

Personal CGSP Number*

Date of Birth

Name (First, MI, Last)
❏ Mr. ❏ Miss
❏ Mrs. ❏

Home Phone

Address (Street, Route, or P.O. Box)

City, State

Zip Code

CHURCH INFORMATION

Church Name

Address (Street, Route, or P. O. Box)

City, State

Zip Code

CHANGE REQUEST ONLY

❏ Former Name

❏ Former Address

City, State

Zip Code

❏ Former Church

Zip Code

Signature of Pastor, Conference Leader, or Other Church Leader

Date

*New participants are requested but not required to give SS# and date of birth. Existing participants, please give CGSP# when using SS# for the first time. Thereafter, only one ID# is required. Mail to: Christian Growth Study Plan, 127 Ninth Ave., North, MSN 117, Nashville, TN 37234-0117. Fax: (615)251-5067